Lectures on the Gospel of John

Footsteps
of the Lord

Volume 2

Dr. Jaerock Lee

Lectures on the Gospel of John

Footsteps
of the Lord

Volume 2

Dr. Jaerock Lee

Footsteps of the Lord: Volume2 by Rev. Jaerock Lee
Published by Urim Books (Representative: Kyungtae Noh)
73, Yeouidaebang-ro 22 Gil, Dongjak-Gu, Seoul, Korea
www.urimbooks.com

Unless otherwise noted, all Scripture quotations are taken from the Holy Bible, NEW AMERICAN STANDARD BIBLE, ®, Copyright © 1960, 1962, 1963, 1968, 1971, 1972, 1973, 1975, 1977, 1995 by The Lockman Foundation. Used by permission.

ISBN: 978-89-7557-754-3, ISBN: 978-89-7557-604-1(set)
Translation Copyright © 2012 by Dr. Esther K. Chung. Used by permission.

First Published May 2013

Previously published in Korean in 2009 by Urim Books in Seoul, Korea

Edited by Dr. Geumsun Vin
Designed by Editorial Bureau of Urim Books
For more information contact: urimbook@hotmail.com

Following In His Footsteps...

While retracing the Lord's footsteps during my pilgrimage to the Holy Land, I came upon the blue waters of the Sea of Galilee. I felt as if I had traveled back 2,000 years to our Lord's time. I could neither pass by one pebble, nor one strand of grass without being awed by its significance. Whenever I closed my eyes for a few seconds, it was like I could clearly hear the Lord's voice. And, while watching the trail of dust rise from behind the feet of the pilgrims taking their steps to follow the Lord's steps, the past and the present became tangled together in one mesh, and I felt as if I was standing in the very place where the Lord carried out His ministry. Perhaps this was due to my earnest desire to follow in His footsteps.

There are Four Gospels in the Bible that trace the steps that the Lord took during His ministry. These Gospels are:

Matthew, Mark, Luke and John. Among the Four Gospels, the Gospel of John, written by John—who was so close to the Lord that he was called "The Beloved Disciple," and who encountered everything firsthand—carries the deepest spiritual significance. It is the Gospel of John that most clearly shows that salvation comes from Jesus Christ alone and that He is the true Son of God.

Every time I read the Gospels, I become overwhelmed with emotions. Especially when I read the Gospel of John, and the Holy Spirit enlightens me with the deep spiritual meaning of the Words recorded in it, I cannot help but share this with everyone I know. Just as the Lord asked the apostle Peter to "Feed My sheep," I also felt compelled to feed all believers with the deep, spiritual secrets found in the Gospel of John. This is why in July of 1990 I began giving the 221 sermon series on the Gospel of John.

Lectures on the Gospel of John: Footsteps of the Lord I & II distinctly capture the image of Jesus from 2,000 years ago, as seen in the eyes of John, who witnessed the life of Jesus firsthand. And passing through the time of eternity, the secrets about the beginning of time, as well as information about the origin of Jesus, and about His love and providence that ultimately led to our salvation, are all unraveled.

Whether He was in the Temple, the meeting place, or the mountains or the fields, Jesus taught the people using illustrations from everyday life so that anyone could easily understand Him. His messages were mainly about God, His duty as the Savior, and eternal life. Even though the high priest or the Pharisees couldn't understand the spiritual meaning of His messages, good people like Nicodemus, the Samaritan woman at the well at Sychar, and Lazarus found new lives through the Lord's messages. While sharing messages of life that couldn't be heard anywhere else, the Lord brought consolation and hope to the sick, the poor, and the neglected. However, those people who refused to understand God's love turned their backs against Jesus, because He was unlike the messiah they were waiting for. And ultimately, these same people shouted for His crucifixion on the cross. Now what do you think was going through Jesus' mind as He hung upon the cross?

When we realize the sacrifice Jesus made—enduring all kinds of pain and torment because the cross was the only way to fulfill God's providence—we can only bow down in humility before Him. From His birth, to the signs and wonders He performed, to the messages He delivered, to His suffering on the cross, and finally to His resurrection, every move Jesus made was significant. When we realize the spiritual meaning behind every incident, we can truly understand the deep love God has for us.

The secret to eternal life that's found in the Gospel of John applies to us today. If we open our hearts and accept the Word with a good heart, we will discover an unbelievable treasure, and if we live according to the Word, God will answer our prayers and give us unbelievable blessings and strength.

I would like to give special thanks to Geumsun Vin, Director of Editorial Bureau and the staff who have so diligently worked hard for the publication of this book, and I hope that everyone who reads this book will experience God's great love. I also pray that as you follow the footsteps of the Lord and live according to His teachings, you will receive the answers to all of your prayers, and that God will bestow upon you incredible blessings from above!

February 2009

Jaerock Lee

How the Gospel of John Came To Be

1. About the Author of the Gospel of John

The author of the Gospel of John is the apostle John. Although there is no mention in the Gospel of John about who its author is, we can easily infer that the author is John. This is because as the Lord's "Beloved Disciple" (John 13:23, 19:26, 20:2, 21:7, 20), John experienced the Lord's life firsthand.

John is the son of Zebedee and Salome, and the younger brother of James. With his brother James, John was one of the first to become Jesus' disciples. Because of his fiery temper, John was called a "Son of Thunder". However, he was so loved by the Lord that He got the chance to witness Jesus' spiritual transformation on the Mount of Transfiguration and the bringing back to life of Jairus' daughter. And after Jesus was captured by the Jews and all the other disciples had fled away in fear, John stayed by the Lord until the moment He died on the cross. And because Jesus saw John's trustworthiness, Jesus entrusted John with the virgin Mary, moments before dying on the cross.

After witnessing Christ's resurrection and receiving the Holy Spirit, John was a changed person. And he dedicated his life to spreading the gospel (Acts 4:13) and spent his last years in Ephesus. Then, during Emperor Domitian's harsh tyranny, John was banished to the Island of Patmos. Made entirely of granite, Patmos Island is a barren land where drinking water is scarce and vegetation can hardly grow.

During the day, under the scrutiny of Roman soldiers, John was forced to work in a quarry under harsh conditions. And during the night, while enduring cold and hunger, John put all his energy into prayer. Even now, if we visit the cave where John is said to have prayed every day, we can still see his handprints that tell us how the conditions were while John was there. After Domitian's death, John returned to Ephesus and died there. In his writings, including the Gospel of John, the First, Second, and Third Epistles of John, and the book of Revelation, John mentions about love over 120 times, which is why he is often called the "Apostle of Love".

2. Why the Gospel of John Was Written

In John 20:31, the apostle John clearly states why he wrote the Gospel of John.

"but these have been written so that you may believe that Jesus is the Christ, the Son of God; and that believing you may have life in His name."

At that time, many Jews hated Jesus and strongly denied that He was the Christ, ultimately killing Him on the cross. But according to what he witnessed firsthand, the apostle John clearly testified that Jesus is the true Son of God, and that He is the Christ.

The theme of the Gospel of John is "Christ, the love, the life, and the Light of the world". And it tells us about the Christ who came to this world to give us life, the Christ who came to light up the world from the darkness, and the Christ who showed God's love to the world by sacrificing Himself.

3. What Makes the Gospel of John so Special

Generally, the three Gospels that record the ministry and teachings of Jesus—Matthew, Mark and Luke—are similar in content, structure, and perspective; which is why these

Gospels are called the Synoptic Gospels. However, there's definitely something that distinguishes the Gospel of John from the other Gospels.

First, the Synoptic Gospels record the ministry of Jesus with Galilee being the main scene of events, but the Gospel of John records the ministry of Jesus focusing mainly on Jerusalem and Judea.

Secondly, although the Passover is only mentioned once in the Synoptic Gospels (Matthew 26:1-5; Mark 14:1; and Luke 22:1-2), the Gospel of John mentions the Passover three times (John 2:13, 6:4, and 11:55), signifying that Jesus' ministry lasted a total of three years.

Thirdly, if the Synoptic Gospels focus on the kingdom of Heaven, the Gospel of John focuses on the relationship between Jesus and God, and eternal life (John 3:16; 5:24, 11:25, 17:2-3).

The Gospel of John explains about the origin of Jesus Christ and how He was with God from the beginning, and the phrase "I am ---" shows up many times throughout the Gospel of John. Phrases like, *"I am the bread of life"* (John 6:35), *"I am the Light of the world"* (John 8:12), *"I am the way and the truth and the life"* (John 14:6), *"I am the good shepherd"* (John 10:11), and *"I am the true vine"* (John

15:1) show clearly who Jesus is. And events like the first sign Jesus performed at the wedding feast in Cana, or His visit to Samaria, and many others that are not recorded in the Synoptic Gospels are recorded in the Gospel of John.

Especially in the Gospel of John, we see a record of how Jesus says, *"Truly, truly, I say to you,"* in many occasions. This strongly emphasizes to the reader the absolute value of God's Word.

Table of Contents

Table of Contents

Chapter 11

Jesus Saves Lazarus

The Death of Lazarus

During His public ministry, Jesus healed all kinds of diseases; even congenital disabilities. Not only that, like the son of the widow from Nain, and the daughter of the synagogue leader Jairus, He even raised dead people back to life again (Luke 7-8).

Jesus even raised a man back to life who had been buried for four days and smelled of decay—Lazarus of Bethany. Jesus always acted according to God's will. And when we look at this event, where He raised Lazarus from the dead, we can discover the special providence of God.

The Family of Lazarus Living in Bethany

"Now a certain man was sick, Lazarus of Bethany, the village of Mary and her sister Martha. It was the Mary who anointed the Lord with ointment, and wiped His feet with her hair, whose brother Lazarus was sick. So the sisters sent word to Him, saying, 'Lord, behold, he whom You love is sick'" (11:1-3).

Approximately 3 kilometers southeast of Jerusalem, in a small town called Bethany, lived two sisters and a brother: Martha, Mary, and Lazarus. Whenever Jesus traveled to Bethany, He often visited their house.

Lazarus' sister, Mary, is well-known as the woman who poured perfume on Jesus' feet. This event actually occurred *after* Lazarus was raised from the dead. However, at the time the Gospel of John was written, this event was widely known, so Mary was introduced as the one "who anointed the Lord with ointment". People sometimes confuse this Mary with Mary Magdalene, but these two are totally different people.

From some moment on, a grave problem arose. Lazarus began to get sick. Even after a long passage of time, instead of getting better, his illness grew worse and worse. Martha and Mary urgently sent a messenger to Jesus, because they knew that Jesus could heal any kind of disease.

"Lord, behold, he whom You love is sick." The messenger that was sent to Jesus did not say who the sick person was. He only called him "he whom You love". Martha and Mary knew that that was all they had to say, and Jesus would know who they meant. By this, we can tell that this family had a very close relationship with Jesus. What could be the cause of this close bond? It was because of Mary, who loved Jesus very much.

Even before Lazarus got sick, Mary loved Jesus and served Him in whatever way she could. In order to repay Him for the grace of showing her the way of truth and eternal life, she sought any kind of work that needed to be done, and diligently served. Witnessing Mary's wonderful transformation, her family also came to love Jesus very much and they too wanted to do whatever they could to serve Him.

After starting His public ministry, Jesus could not even eat or rest comfortably. He was always surrounded by many people, and He did not have a chance to rest even a little while. Knowing this, Mary and her siblings always wondered, "How can we make Jesus more comfortable?" So whenever Jesus was near their house, they invited Him to their house and served Him as best as they could (Luke 10:38).

They believed that Jesus was God's Son, and they shared everything with Him. They served Him and loved Him without expecting anything in return, and Jesus knew it. Jesus loved them very much as well. Mary's family loved Jesus and received His love too. This was this family's key to receiving God's grace and blessings. The event of Lazarus dying, his sisters calling for Jesus, and Lazarus coming back to life, didn't just happen by chance.

Jesus Hears About Lazarus' Illness

"But when Jesus heard this, He said, 'This sickness is not to end in death, but for the glory of God, so that the Son of God may be glorified by it.' Now Jesus loved Martha and her sister and Lazarus. So when He heard that he was sick, He then stayed two days longer in the place where He was" (11:4-6).

While baptizing at the Jordan River, Jesus heard that the one He loved was sick. But Jesus responded to this message as if He already knew about it.

"This sickness is not to end in death..." Even though Jesus heard that Lazarus was gravely sick, He didn't hurry to go; instead, He stayed where He was for two more days. This action may seem a bit cold, but Jesus was waiting for God's time. He knew that through this event, Lazarus would give glory to God, and that it would be glory for Jesus Himself to make it happen.

In Numbers 16:22, it is written, *"God of the spirits of all flesh,"* and in Psalm 36:9 it says, *"For with You is the fountain of life."* The book of Acts 17:25 records the following about God, *"He Himself gives to all people life and breath and all things."* Every man's life is in God's hands, and only God is the author of life and death. But if a person was to bring back another person from the dead, wouldn't that be strange? A mere man cannot imitate—let alone even imagine—doing something like that!

With the power of being one with God, Jesus knew that

someday, in front of many witnesses, He would be raising Lazarus from the dead. He also knew that through this event, He would show that He is the Son of God, who is the author of life and death, and that many people would come to believe that He is the Christ. That is why Jesus said, "This sickness is not to end in death, but for the glory of God, so that the Son of God may be glorified by it," and then waited for God's time.

"Are there not twelve hours in the day?"

"Then after this He said to the disciples, 'Let us go to Judea again.' The disciples said to Him, 'Rabbi, the Jews were just now seeking to stone You, and are You going there again?' Jesus answered, 'Are there not twelve hours in the day? If anyone walks in the day, he does not stumble, because he sees the light of this world. 'But if anyone walks in the night, he stumbles, because the light is not in him'" (11:7-10).

Two days after receiving the news from Bethany, Jesus said, "Let us go to Judea again." Judea, the southern region of Palestine, not only includes Jerusalem and Bethlehem, but also Bethany, the place where Lazarus lived. Hearing the word "Judea", the disciples became alarmed, and asked, "Rabbi, the Jews were just now seeking to stone You, and are You going there again?"

The reason the disciples hesitated, was because just days prior to that, during the Feast of the Dedication, the Jews had tried to stone Jesus. When Jesus said, "I and the Father are one," the angry Jews had picked up stones to stone Jesus (John 10:22-31). Because it was not God's time yet, no one could capture Jesus any way, but because the disciples had this one experience, they were worried. Jesus knew what was troubling them.

Jesus then gave the nervous disciples an answer they did not expect, saying "Are there not twelve hours in the day? If anyone walks in the day, he does not stumble, because he sees the light of this world. But if anyone walks in the night, he stumbles, because the light is not in him."

This may seem like a random answer at first, but there are two spiritual meanings behind this statement that Jesus made.

The first meaning is that Jesus still has some time left to work. He is letting them know that it is not yet time for Him to be captured and nailed to the cross. To the Jewish people, "one day" is from dawn of one day until dawn of the next day. Back then, in Judea, one hour was not defined as 60 minutes yet. One hour was the day time divided by 12. Since the day time was different depending on the season, the day was longer in the summer and shorter in the winter. So during the shortest day, one hour could be about 49 mintues, and during the longest day, about 71 minutes.

Because the day time was divided by 12, whether it be short or long, for the Jews, a day always consisted of twelve hours. So when Jesus asked, "Are there not twelve hours in the day?" He was telling them that there was still some time left to work. "Day" is when the light is shining. In 1 John 1:5 it says, *"God is Light, and in Him there is no darkness at all."* So the time, which God, who is the Light, entrusted to Jesus, was still left. To the disciples who were worried, thinking, "What if Jesus is captured? What if people try to stone Him?"Jesus was teaching them that because God was watching and protecting Him, no matter how hard they tried the Jews could not capture Him.

Secondly, Jesus' statement also signifies that in accordance with God's will, Jesus would be raising dead Lazarus back to life without fail. The disciples did not know, but because Jesus abided with God, He already knew the outcome of His work. God has absolutely no darkness in Him so spiritually light refers to God. We do not misstep or slip when moving around in the day. Likewise, when we live in the midst of God's Word—the truth—we can only be safe. Jesus, who always followed God's will, never made a faulty step. And by raising Lazarus back to life, He fulfilled God's will and providence.

No matter how dangerous the situation may have seemed, because Jesus walked in the day, meaning He did everything according to God's will, He was safe. So, on the contrary, if we fear man, and we do not act according to God's will, it is like walking in the night; therefore we could make missteps and fall into a snare.

"Lazarus Has Fallen Asleep..."

"This He said, and after that He said to them, 'Our friend Lazarus has fallen asleep; but I go, so that I may awaken him out of sleep.' The disciples then said to Him, 'Lord, if he has fallen asleep, he will recover.' Now Jesus had spoken of his death, but they thought that He was speaking of literal sleep" (11:11-13).

After reassuring the disciples who were afraid of going back to the region of Judea, Jesus said, "Our friend Lazarus has fallen asleep; but I go, so that I may awaken him out of sleep." This is how He told them why He needed to go back there. When a messenger came to Jesus two days prior asking Him to heal Lazarus, Jesus did not have much to say. But now He was saying He needed to go and wake him up. The disciples were pretty confused. They were probably thinking, "He didn't even go when the man was sick. And now He is saying He is going to wake up a sleeping man." Now Jesus was referring to Lazarus' death; but the disciples were trying to understand the situation just by looking at the surface. They did not grasp the spiritual meaning of Jesus' words.

"Lord, if he has fallen asleep, he will recover." People usually think that what they see with their eyes is everything. But because Jesus knew God's will, He thought differently. Even though Lazarus was dead, He knew that he would come back to life again. That is why He said, "He is asleep, I will wake him up."

"Let Us Go To Him"

"So Jesus then said to them plainly, 'Lazarus is dead,

and I am glad for your sakes that I was not there, so that you may believe; but let us go to him.' Therefore Thomas, who is called Didymus, said to his fellow disciples, 'Let us also go, so that we may die with Him'" (11:14-16).

To the disciples who still did not understand Him, Jesus plainly said, "Lazarus is dead." They knew what the real situation was. This was so that when they did get to Bethany, they could have faith when He raised Lazarus from the dead.

What would have happened if Jesus went to Bethany the moment He heard the news about Lazarus? Even if Lazarus was healed, the people would not have believed that it was the work of God. They probably would have believed that it was by chance that he recovered. They might have thought it was a trick, or some temporary phenomenon. Furthermore, if Lazarus had died while Jesus was there, someone probably would have secretly picked it as a point for an argument.

With the given situation, Jesus knew exactly when He needed to act to show God's power. That is why He waited for God's exact appointed time to go to Bethany to raise up Lazarus, who had been dead for four days.

The Jews back then believed that when a person dies, the person's soul wanders around the tomb for three days and then leaves. But in Lazarus' case, it was four days since his death, so the people did not even think that he could come back to life. However, as it is written in John 5:21, *"For just as the Father raises the dead and gives them life, even so the Son also gives life to whom He wishes,"* in accordance with God's will, Jesus,

God's Son, could raise a dead person and restore life to him.

After announcing Lazarus' death, Jesus said, "Let us go to Judea." Thomas, one of the disciples, made a random comment saying, "Let us also go, so that we may die with Him." On one hand, it seems like he is courageously risking his life for Jesus, but in a spiritual sense, this is a sad reply. Jesus specifically told the disciples that Lazarus' illness would show God's glory; but he still did not understand.

If Thomas had grasped the spiritual meaning behind Jesus' words, he would have said, "Let us also go, so that we may witness God's glory." The reason why God allowed Thomas' confession to be recorded in the Bible was so that we, who are reading about it today, could check to see if we are like Thomas in any way, and learn from him. It was not to bring Thomas' weakness out into the open.

While travelling with Jesus, Thomas heard the words of truth and witnessed God's power on many occasions. He saw all kinds of diseases being healed, he saw the sign of the two fish and five loaves, and he even saw Jesus walking on the water. However, because he did not have true faith, in the moment of truth when he really needed to show his faith, he ended up making a confession which showed his lack of faith. Even though Thomas knew that Jesus had great power and that God was with Him, because he had not yet had a spiritual awakening, he made a confession based on reasoning of the flesh.

Lazarus Walks
Out of the Tomb

After hearing the news of Lazarus' death, many Jews came to comfort Martha and Mary. On the fourth day from the time Lazarus was put into the tomb, Jesus came to bring life back to him.

Bethany is a town very close to Jerusalem in proximity. Therefore many of the Jews had come from Jerusalem. These same Jews witnessed Lazarus coming back to life. Among these Jews, some of them were actually hostile toward Jesus.

"Your Brother Will Rise Again"

"So when Jesus came, He found that he had already been in the tomb four days. Now Bethany was near

Jerusalem, about two miles off; and many of the Jews had come to Martha and Mary, to console them concerning their brother. Martha therefore, when she heard that Jesus was coming, went to meet Him, but Mary stayed at the house. Martha then said to Jesus, 'Lord, if You had been here, my brother would not have died. Even now I know that whatever You ask of God, God will give You.' Jesus said to her, 'Your brother will rise again.' Martha said to Him, 'I know that he will rise again in the resurrection on the last day'" (11:17-24).

Four days after Lazarus died, Jesus arrived at Bethany, where Lazarus had lived. Someone sent Martha a message saying, "Jesus is coming." With the sorrow of losing a loved one, she was probably in no mood to move about; but when she heard that Jesus was coming, she rushed out to greet Him.

The funeral was over. Everything was done. When Martha came out to meet Jesus, what kind of state of mind do you think she was in?

"Lord, if You had been here, my brother would not have died." Martha loved Jesus, so she was always very interested in hearing about the things that Jesus did to give glory to God. Since Jesus had the power to heal all kinds of diseases and infirmities, she thought that if He had been here before Lazarus died, Lazarus would not have died.

But the reality of the situation was not so simple as Lazarus

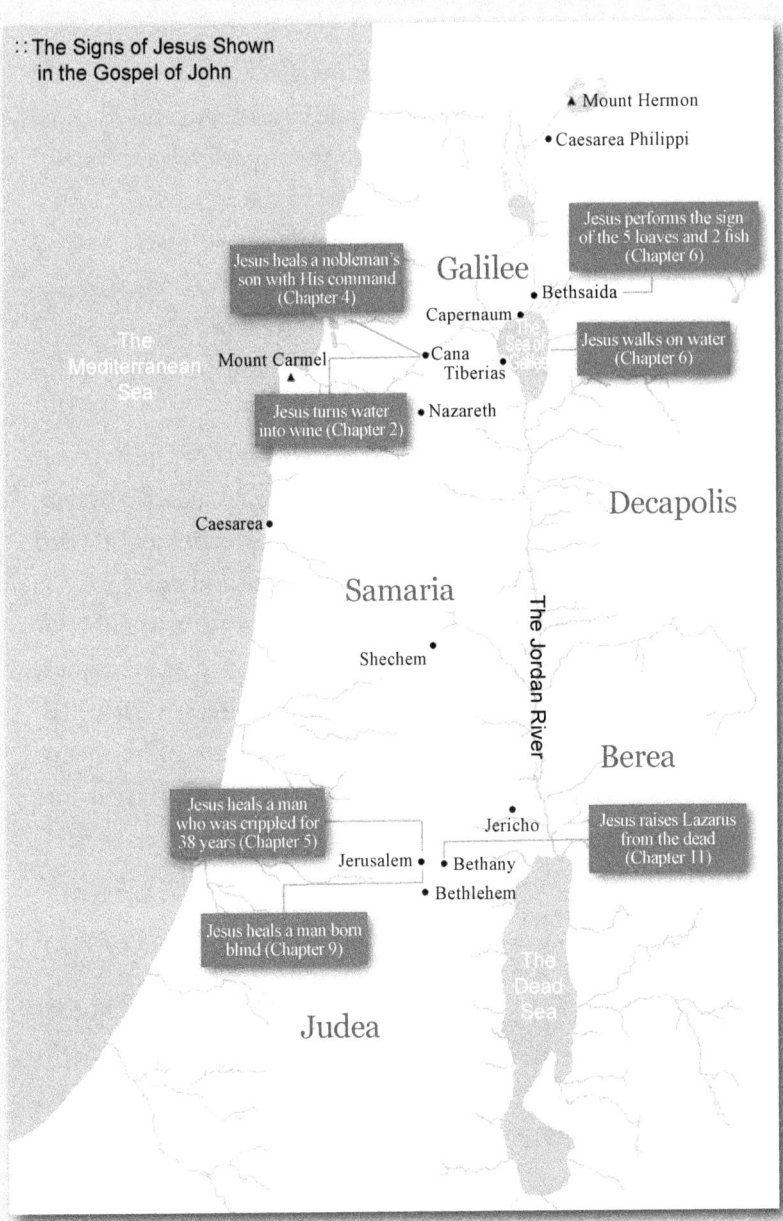

:: The Signs of Jesus Shown in the Gospel of John

Mount Hermon

Caesarea Philippi

Galilee

Jesus performs the sign of the 5 loaves and 2 fish (Chapter 6)

Jesus heals a nobleman's son with His command (Chapter 4)

Bethsaida

Capernaum

The Sea of Galilee

Jesus walks on water (Chapter 6)

The Mediterranean Sea

Mount Carmel

Cana
Tiberias

Jesus turns water into wine (Chapter 2)

Nazareth

Decapolis

Caesarea

Samaria

Shechem

The Jordan River

Berea

Jesus heals a man who was crippled for 38 years (Chapter 5)

Jericho

Jerusalem

Bethany

Jesus raises Lazarus from the dead (Chapter 11)

Bethlehem

Jesus heals a man born blind (Chapter 9)

The Dead Sea

Judea

just being sick. He had been dead for four days, and his body already smelled from decay. With the given circumstances, no one in the world would even imagine that Lazarus could come back to life. However, Martha made an unexpected confession.

"Even now I know that whatever You ask of God, God will give You." In reality, Martha did not say this because she thought Lazarus was coming back to life—because since the beginning of creation, no one had ever heard of a man who came back to life after dying and decaying for four days. But trusting and having faith in God, Martha was confessing that Jesus could make anything happen. Although Martha was in a truly tough and sad situation, her confession, which showed her trust and faith in Jesus, was very beautiful and precious.

If there was already an event prior to this time where Jesus had raised a man that was dead for four days, and Martha knew about it, of course she would have shown greater faith than this. But seeing this kind of faith in the center of her heart, nonetheless, Jesus leads Martha to a higher level of faith that surpasses even death, by saying, "Your brother will rise again."

To this, Martha answered, "I know that he will rise again in the resurrection on the last day."

Martha did not deny Jesus' words. But upon hearing that Lazarus would come back to life even now, because she could not have imagined this based on her knowledge and reasoning, she made this spiritual statement with the limited knowledge that she had.

As it is written in John 5:28-29, *"For an hour is coming, in*

which all who are in the tombs will hear His voice, and will
come forth; those who did the good deeds to a resurrection of
life, those who committed the evil deeds to a resurrection of
judgment," wherever He went, Jesus taught the people about
the resurrection and the judgment when preaching about the
gospel of the kingdom of heaven.

This is why when Jesus said, "Your brother will rise again,"
Martha said that she knew Lazarus would resurrect on the
last day. However, her confession was based on knowledge,
not true, spiritual faith. But Martha was not alone. Most of
the people who believed in Jesus, including His disciples, all
thought the same way.

Those who heard about the resurrection on the last day all
had knowledge it, but almost none of them had spiritual faith
about it. That is why Jesus decided to show them the power of
God that could even raise Lazarus from the dead. He knew that
it just takes one experience to help a person with a good heart
gain complete faith and hope for the resurrection.

"I Am the Resurrection and the Life"

"Jesus said to her, 'I am the resurrection and the life;
he who believes in Me will live even if he dies, and
everyone who lives and believes in Me will never die.
Do you believe this?' She said to Him, 'Yes, Lord; I
have believed that You are the Christ, the Son of God,
even He who comes into the world'" (11:25-27).

When Martha said, "I know Lazarus will resurrect on the last day," Jesus answered, "I am the resurrection and the life; he who believes in Me will live even if he dies, and everyone who lives and believes in Me will never die. Do you believe this?"

When Martha answered "Amen" to this without incorporating her flesh thoughts into it, her faith could be considered one level above the rest, and this is the faith that would get her prayer answered. This is because Jesus, who is the resurrection and the life, is standing in front of her. Because Jesus is completely one with God, who is the one and only author of life, He could raise a dead person to life. That is why Jesus said, "I am the resurrection and the life; he who believes in Me will live even if he dies," so that Martha could believe in this truth.

Jesus also meant through this phrase that those who believe and receive Jesus as their Savior and Lord have the promise of eternal life. When a person believes in Jesus Christ and is forgiven of his sins, the Holy Spirit comes upon him and his spirit, which was dead, comes back to life. This is called "spiritual resurrection", and this is only possible through Jesus Christ. Originally, when man was created, he had a living spirit. But when the first man, Adam, sinned, his spirit died. So, all of his descendants after him also had spirits that were dead. However, for those who receive Jesus Christ and are forgiven of their sins, the Holy Spirit enters their hearts and revives the spirit, and it comes back to life.

That is why as Jesus said, "Everyone who lives and believes in Me will never die," for anyone who is a child of God, even if his physical body dies, his spirit lives on and lives eternally in

Heaven. In the last day, when the Lord returns in the air, bodies that were decaying in the tomb will resurrect and transform into immortal bodies. This is called "resurrection of the body". This resurrection of the body is only possible through Jesus Christ. That is why He said "I am the resurrection."

Just moments before this, Martha simply had an indefinite reliance on Jesus, but after listening to His words, she made a definite confession of her faith: "I have believed that You are the Christ, the Son of God, even He who comes into the world."

Mary Falls at Jesus' Feet

"When she had said this, she went away and called Mary her sister, saying secretly, 'The Teacher is here and is calling for you.' And when she heard it, she got up quickly and was coming to Him. Now Jesus had not yet come into the village, but was still in the place where Martha met Him. Then the Jews who were with her in the house, and consoling her, when they saw that Mary got up quickly and went out, they followed her, supposing that she was going to the tomb to weep there. Therefore, when Mary came where Jesus was, she saw Him, and fell at His feet, saying to Him, 'Lord, if You had been here, my brother would not have died'" (11:28-32).

After being spiritually enlightened, Martha returned to her

house and said to her sister, "The Teacher is here and is calling for you." Then Mary quickly got up and ran to Jesus. The Jews who were consoling her thought she was going to mourn at the tomb, so they followed her. Jesus had not come into the village yet. He was still at the place where He had met Martha. As soon as she saw Jesus, Mary fell at His feet weeping mournfully and making the same confession as her sister, "Lord, if You had been here, my brother would not have died."

> "**When Jesus therefore saw her weeping, and the Jews who came with her also weeping, He was deeply moved in spirit and was troubled, and said, 'Where have you laid him?' They said to Him, 'Lord, come and see.' Jesus wept. So the Jews were saying, 'See how He loved him!' But some of them said, 'Could not this man, who opened the eyes of the blind man, have kept this man also from dying?'" (11:33-37).**

When Mary cried, the Jews who followed her wept with empathy; people sniffled here and there. Seeing those who had no faith, Jesus felt the sorrow too. But, seeing Mary cry at His feet, He felt her sorrow and wept with her. This scene shows us Jesus' love.

Jesus came into this world and experienced the joys and pains of life with mankind. When people shed tears and mourned, Jesus felt their pain. When He saw the blind, He felt their suffering. That is why He had mercy on them and opened their eyes. He reached out in love and healed the lepers, who were rejected by other people. But the Jews who saw Jesus cry all had different reactions.

"See how He loved him!"
"Could not this man, who opened the eyes of the blind man, have kept this man also from dying?"
Some thought Jesus must have really loved Lazarus. Some wondered why He could open the eyes of the blind, but couldn't save Lazarus from dying.

"Remove the Stone"

> "So Jesus, again being deeply moved within, came to the tomb. Now it was a cave, and a stone was lying against it. Jesus said, 'Remove the stone.' Martha, the sister of the deceased, said to Him, 'Lord, by this time there will be a stench, for he has been dead four days.' Jesus said to her, 'Did I not say to you that if you believe, you will see the glory of God?'" (11:38-40).

Jesus knew what was in everyone's heart. Having pity on them, He went to the tomb. Many people had gathered at Lazarus' tomb to comfort Martha and Mary. In Israel back then, caves were used as tombs. The dead body was placed in the cave, and a large stone covered the opening of the cave. In order to bring out Lazarus, who was dead, Jesus commanded one thing. "Remove the stone."

Martha, who couldn't understand Jesus' words, replied in shock, "Lord, by this time there will be a stench, for he has been dead four days." Jesus answered, "Did I not say to you that if you believe, you will see the glory of God?"

Martha did make a confession of her faith at the entrance to her village, where she greeted Jesus, but the reality of her circumstances did not change. Because God works in strict adherence to the spiritual law, even Jesus, the Son of God, cannot just bless anyone at random. The person receiving the blessing must meet the necessary requirements to receive the blessing. That is why they needed to remove the stone; to show their faith through physical action.

Since dead Lazarus could not show his faith, Jesus led his family members to show their faith for him—through their acts of obedience. No matter how much authority and power Jesus may have, and even if Lazarus was chosen to show God's glory, if it was not in God's will, nothing would have happened.

Therefore, so they would believe and depend on Jesus, He told Lazarus' family 'if you believe, you will see God's glory.' Thereby they could satisfy all the conditions they needed to experience God's power.

"Lazarus, Come Forth"

"So they removed the stone. Then Jesus raised His eyes, and said, 'Father, I thank You that You have heard Me. I knew that You always hear Me; but because of the people standing around I said it, so that they may believe that You sent Me.' When He had said these

:: Lazarus' stone tomb, located in the basement of the Church of Saint Lazarus

things, He cried out with a loud voice, 'Lazarus, come forth.' The man who had died came forth, bound hand and foot with wrappings, and his face was wrapped around with a cloth. Jesus said to them, 'Unbind him, and let him go'" (11:41-44).

Once Lazarus' family members moved the stone away from the entrance to the cave, all the people's eyes focused on Jesus. "What's He going to do now?" Everyone wondered and held their breath in suspense. At that moment Jesus lifted His eyes to the sky and made this confession: "Father, I thank You that You have heard Me. I knew that You always hear Me; but because of the people standing around I said it, so that they may believe that You sent Me." The reason Jesus made this confession at a moment when everyone looked upon Him in suspense, was so that He could lead as many people as possible to have faith and receive salvation.

Shortly after that, Jesus called out in a loud voice, "Lazarus, come forth!" People could not believe that Jesus was telling a dead man to come out. But something incredible happened. Lazarus, who had been dead, came walking out! His hands and feet bound by burial wrappings, and his face covered with cloth, Lazarus walked out. The people gathered there were so shocked they didn't know what to say. As they stood in astonishment, they heard Jesus speak again: "Unbind him, and let him go."

How could a dead person that has already begun to decay come back to life, just because Jesus calls him? This is possible because God guaranteed Jesus' very word one hundred percent. God the Creator, the Lord of all the universe and author of life and death was with Him, therefore no matter what command Jesus gave, anything and everything in creation had to obey Him.

The Conspiracy to Kill Jesus

When Lazarus came back to life, how joyful Mary and Martha must have been! They probably couldn't forget this grace during the rest of their lives! But this was not just a significant event for Lazarus and his family. Many Jews who actually witnessed this event came to believe in Jesus as their Messiah.

However, the high priest, Pharisees, and all the Jews with power still had no interest in the good works of Jesus. They tried whatever they could to find fault with Him, and conspired to kill Him.

The People Who Convened a Council

"Therefore many of the Jews who came to Mary, and

saw what He had done, believed in Him. But some of them went to the Pharisees and told them the things which Jesus had done. Therefore the chief priests and the Pharisees convened a council, and were saying, 'What are we doing? For this man is performing many signs. If we let Him go on like this, all men will believe in Him, and the Romans will come and take away both our place and our nation'" (11:45-48).

Many Jews who witnessed firsthand the event of Lazarus coming back to life came to believe in Jesus. Even though it was hard not to believe after witnessing such undeniable evidence of God, there were some people who went to the Pharisees to tell them what happened. The moment they heard this news, the high priests and Pharisees immediately convened a council and discussed this event.

"For this man is performing many signs. If we let Him go on like this, all men will believe in Him, and the Romans will come and take away both our place and our nation."

They knew that many people believed in Jesus and following Him because He was performing many signs. On top of that, He even raised a man who had been dead for four days, back to life again! It was clear as day that even more people would come to believe in Him and follow Him. Many people believed that Jesus was the prophesied Messiah, and that He would save them from Roman oppression, and guarantee them safety and prosperity. They thought of Jesus both as their Savior *and* political leader, or king.

It was feared that if a king had truly emerged—as the people expected—and many people began following him, the Roman government would probably increase their military power and oppress Israel even more. Then the status of the high priest and the Pharisees, whose power and authority were sheltered by the Roman government, would become unstable. So when the high priest and the Pharisees felt as though their freedom and authority were in jeopardy, they thought that Jesus was the cause of all their problems.

Through many circumstances, they came to realize that Jesus was an extraordinary person. That is why they hired people to spy on Him, and then report back every little thing that Jesus did. And unable to believe that He was the Son of God, they only considered Him as someone who was threatening their power and authority. So no matter how many good things Jesus did, they were not interested in those works. Using the laws and the tradition of the elders, they tried only to find some kind of fault in Jesus, and conspired to kill Him somehow.

The High Priest Prophecies Jesus' Death

"But one of them, Caiaphas, who was high priest that year, said to them, 'You know nothing at all, nor do you take into account that it is expedient for you that one man die for the people, and that the whole nation not perish.' Now he did not say this on his own initiative, but being high priest that year, he prophesied that Jesus was going to die for the nation, and not for the nation only, but in order that He might also gather together into one the children of God who are scattered abroad" (11:49-52).

After Lazarus' resurrection, the Jews who gathered to come up with some kind of plan were all full of opinions but no real solution. At that time, Caiaphas, the high priest, spoke up: "You know nothing at all, nor do you take into account that it is expedient for you that one man die for the people, and that the whole nation not perish."

These words contain the implication that through the righteous act of the sinless Jesus who died on the cross many people can be led to gain life. So through this, we can see that Jesus' death was going to occur, not because He is a sinner, or because He led many people astray, but solely as part of God's divine providence.

Romans 5:18-19 says, *"So then as through one transgression there resulted condemnation to all men, even so through one act of righteousness there resulted justification of life to all men. For as through the one man's disobedience the many were made sinners, even so through the obedience of the One the many will be made righteous."* Also, as it is stated in Galatians 3:28, *"There is neither Jew nor Greek, there is neither slave nor free man, there is neither male nor female; for you are all one in Christ Jesus,"* Jesus' death was for people of all nations, according to God's providence.

However, Caiaphas didn't really know the true meaning behind his own words. So, why did God have the high priest, who was the leading man behind such strong opposition against Jesus, make this kind of prophecy? This was because the words of the high priest had such a great impact in those days. People listened to what he said, and held his words in their hearts.

If the high priest had spoken according to his own will, he probably would have said, "Let's quickly capture this Jesus, get rid of Him, and save our nation!" But even at that moment, God controlled his lips. The high priest spoke with the intention of telling the people that they needed to capture Jesus and kill Him, but God made His providence show through his words. Likewise, we may think we plan and speak many things on our own accord, but all things occur according to God's method and providence, which far surpass man's wisdom.

As soon as the high priest said that the death of the one man, Jesus, would benefit the whole nation, the conspiracy to kill Jesus began to roll out with full force. These people did not intend to kill Jesus from the very beginning. At first, they were just pierced in their hearts because Jesus pointed out the evil in their hearts. The problem is what happened afterwards. They should have come to a realization and repented right after they were reprimanded the first time; but instead, they continued to pile up more sins. They denied that the signs and wonders that Jesus performed were the works of God, but they rather accused Jesus of being demon-possessed, and thereby they spoke and acted against the Holy Spirit.

As it is written in James 1:15, *"Then when lust has conceived, it gives birth to sin; and when sin is accomplished, it brings forth death,"* because they did not cast out their evil thoughts, evil words and actions came out of them repeatedly; and finally, they ended up going to the way of eternal death, where they could not receive salvation.

The People Who Sought to Capture Jesus

"So from that day on they planned together to kill Him. Therefore Jesus no longer continued to walk publicly among the Jews, but went away from there to the country near the wilderness, into a city called Ephraim; and there He stayed with the disciples. Now the Passover of the Jews was near, and many went up to Jerusalem out of the country before the Passover to purify themselves. So they were seeking for Jesus, and were saying to one another as they stood in the temple, 'What do you think; that He will not come to the feast at all?' Now the chief priests and the Pharisees had given orders that if anyone knew where He was, he was to report it, so that they might seize Him" (11:53-57).

Jesus knew that the conspiracy to kill Him had begun in earnest. In the region of Judea, there was already a decree from the high priests and the Pharisees that stated, 'Anyone who knows the whereabouts of Jesus should report it so He can be captured.' This is why Jesus went to Ephraim, about 20 kilometers north of Jerusalem. And He stayed there with His disciples until the Passover. Because the Passover was such a big holiday, all the people of Israel went to Jerusalem to celebrate it. However, anyone who came in contact with a defiled or unclean animal or object, or who committed an unclean act could not participate in the Passover celebration.

So during the time of Passover, Jerusalem was already bustling with people. In the temple of Jerusalem, people were clustered here and there holding conversations. For the most part, the topic of their conversation was Jesus. Moreover, some people fought through the crowds to look for Jesus, and talk of Jesus blossomed all over the place. "What do you think?" "Do you think that He might not come to the feast at all?"

With the given circumstances, it was probably easy for the people to think that Jesus would not come up to Jerusalem for fear of being captured. However, this was no more than mere human thoughts. Jesus did not think this way. One who truly loves God will put everything in His hands and depend on Him.

Matthew 10:28 reads, *"Do not fear those who kill the body but are unable to kill the soul; but rather fear Him who is able to destroy both soul and body in hell."*

Chapter 12

The Victorious Entry
Into Jerusalem

1. Mary Prepares for Jesus' Burial
(12:1-11)

2. The Entrance into Jerusalem
(12:12-36)

3. The Teaching of the Messiah
(12:37-50)

Mary Prepares for Jesus' Burial

With the Passover just days away, it was also the last week of Jesus' somewhat short three years of public ministry. Knowing both the Jews' plot to kill Him, and the Father God's will and providence of salvation by His death on the cross, this time was unlike any other time for Jesus. When it was time for the Passover, Jesus broke all the people's expectations and went back to Bethany, where Lazarus' family lived. Even though He knew the dangers that lay waiting for Him there, He appeared before the Jews, in order to fulfill God's will. But even with such tension in the air, there were those who prepared a feast for Jesus.

Mary of Bethany Pours Perfume On Jesus' Feet

"Jesus, therefore, six days before the Passover, came to Bethany where Lazarus was, whom Jesus had raised from the dead. So they made Him a supper there, and Martha was serving; but Lazarus was one of those reclining at the table with Him. Mary then took a pound of very costly perfume of pure nard, and anointed the feet of Jesus and wiped His feet with her hair; and the house was filled with the fragrance of the perfume" (12:1-3).

When they heard the news that Jesus was coming to Bethany, Lazarus' family prepared a large feast for Him. Martha was very busy preparing food for the guests. It was a very festive atmosphere; and the people were reliving the excitement of when Lazarus was brought back to life from the dead. Jesus, who was the honorary guest of the evening, sat down to dine together with His disciples and Lazarus.

At that moment, Mary, holding a very expensive jar of perfume, came to Jesus' side. Then she poured the perfume on His feet. The fragrance of the perfume of pure nard filled the house. In contrast to the people who were looking on Mary's actions with surprise and curiosity, Mary was very solemn. After pouring the perfume, she bowed down and wiped Jesus' feet with her hair.

In those days, for a woman to wash someone's feet with her hair was unimaginable. On top of that, to wash someone's feet meant that you were of the lowest class. But to Mary, it was not about what people saw or thought. To Mary, it was not about the expensive perfume. For Mary, it was about doing whatever she could do to express the true love and appreciation she had in her heart to Jesus for raising Lazarus from the dead. When we look at the spiritual symbolism of the jar and perfume, we can better understand what a beautiful thing it was that Mary did.

A 'jar' back then was a container for very valuable goods or treasure. It did not have a top or a cover. In order to get the perfume out, one had to break the opening of the jar. A 'jar' symbolizes the body. So when Mary broke the jar, it showed that she was sacrificing her body in order to serve the Lord. Like Mary, only when we put aside our status or position, and the worries about what other people might think of us, and surrender ourselves, can we truly serve the Lord.

'Nard' is a special type of plant that grows in the Himalayas. It is not only rare; but also the process of turning it into perfume is quite difficult. One pound of pure nard would have cost about three hundred denarii. One denarius was worth a day's wage. So three hundred denarii was a large sum of money, equivalent to one year's worth of wages—and that is after a laborer saved without spending any of it.

This is how valuable the perfume was, which Mary poured upon Jesus' feet. She was giving everything she had, and everything she was, to the Lord. What Mary did was beautiful. That's why to this day, whenever we read about what Mary did, we can still smell the same beautiful fragrance within our hearts.

Judas Iscariot Criticizes Mary

But one of Jesus' disciples who was intending to betray Him, Judas Iscariot, said, 'Why was this perfume not sold for three hundred denarii and given to poor people?' Now he said this, not because he was concerned about the poor, but because he was a thief, and as he had the money box, he used to pilfer what was put into it. Therefore Jesus said, 'Let her alone, so that she may keep it for the day of My burial. For you always have the poor with you, but you do not always have Me'" (12:4-8).

When people saw this scene, they began to talk. Some were surprised by her unexpected action, and some talked amongst themselves, wondering, "Why is she doing that?" Just then, Judas Iscariot gave a disapproving look and criticized Mary. He scolded her for wasting the expensive perfume, instead of using it to help the poor. At first, it seems like what he's saying is right. However, Judas Iscariot's heart was not in the right place when he said what he did.

As one of Jesus' disciples, he managed the finances. Often times, he helped himself to some of the money he was supposed to manage. If Mary had sold the perfume and given the money to Jesus, Judas could have taken a goodly amount of that money for himself. The more he thought about the perfume being poured on Jesus' feet, the more he craved for that money he could have had. To Judas Iscariot's criticism, Jesus replied, "Let her alone, so that she may keep it for the day of My burial. For you always have the poor with you, but you do not always have Me."

In Mark 14:8, we can see what Jesus said about what Mary did, *"She has done what she could; she has anointed My body beforehand for the burial."* And just as He said, a few days later, Jesus died on the cross. Of course Mary didn't pour the perfume on Him knowing that would happen—she loved Him, and lived a life for Him, so she was just moved to express that love to Him.

So as a result, Mary played the important role of preparing for His burial ahead of time. And for this reason, Jesus spoke the following about Mary, *"Truly I say to you, wherever the gospel is preached in the whole world, what this woman has done will also be spoken of in memory of her"* (Mark 14:9). This made Mary become a very blessed woman.

Judas Iscariot, on the other hand, was already frustrated about the perfume. But when Jesus stood up for Mary, he became even angrier. He felt as though his words were disrespected. He even felt that he should no longer be with Jesus any more. While being with Jesus, he saw many signs and wonders that cannot be done by man. Then why does he end up making Jesus grieve and say that it would have been better if Judas had not been born at all (Matthew 26:24)?

On the outside, Judas Iscariot looked like he was following Jesus and helping Him. But deep inside of his heart, he was greedy and selfish. As the treasurer, he noticed that the amount of offerings that came in from people who received God's grace through Jesus was quite a large sum. Even when he helped himself to some of the money, nobody knew. Driven by his own greed, he continued to steal from the money bag and did not change his ways. And as one of Jesus' disciples, he knew he would be respected, and he even put into calculation that if Jesus became a powerful leader, he too, would partake in some of that power.

But the circumstances kept deviating from his expectations. Jesus kept becoming the high priests' and Pharisees' object of hate and condemnation. No one knew when He could be captured. On top of that, Jesus was defending Mary's actions, provoking Judas into further resentment. The emotions of disappointment and frustration grew deeper and deeper for Judas. This is when he decided to turn Jesus over to the high priests, and from then on, he kept looking for the right opportunity to betray Jesus (Matthew 26:14-16).

The Chief Priests Also Plan to Kill Lazarus

"The large crowd of the Jews then learned that He was there; and they came, not for Jesus' sake only, but that they might also see Lazarus, whom He raised from the dead. But the chief priests planned to put Lazarus to death also; because on account of him many of the Jews were going away and were believing in Jesus" (12:9-11).

On their way up to Jerusalem to prepare for the Passover, many people began to crowd into nearby Bethany because they heard that Jesus was there. They wanted to see firsthand who this Jesus was, who raised a dead person that was in the tomb for four days.

Raising a person who was in the grave for four days was evidence that helped people trust in Jesus even more. If God had not been with Jesus, this kind of evidence could not have occured. But even after seeing this kind of evidence, the high priests refused to believe. And because many Jews began to believe and follow Jesus on account of Lazarus, they even planned to kill Lazarus. Like people who have eyes but cannot see, and ears but cannot hear; because their hearts were wicked, they saw God's power but they neither knew, nor understood the truth.

The Entrance into Jerusalem

In order to go to Jerusalem, Jesus, who was in Bethany with His disciples, had to pass by Bethphage, located at the foot of the southeastern side of the Mount of Olives. With Passover approaching, He was going up to Jerusalem to fulfill His mission on the cross. Because the entrance into Jerusalem is depicted very briefly in the Gospel of John, we will also use Matthew chapter 21 and Mark chapter 11 as references.

The People Shout "Hosanna!" While Welcoming Jesus

"On the next day the large crowd who had come to the feast, when they heard that Jesus was coming to Jerusalem, took the branches of the palm trees and went out to meet Him, and began to shout, 'Hosanna! Blessed is He who comes in the name of the Lord, even the King of Israel.' Jesus, finding a young donkey, sat on it; as it is written..." (12:12-14).

Right before entering Jerusalem, Jesus told two of His disciples to go to the village on the opposite side and bring a young donkey from there (Mark chapter 11). Knowing the disciples would wonder, "Why does He want us to bring a donkey all of a sudden?" Jesus told them: *"If anyone says to you, 'Why are you doing this?' you say, 'The Lord has need of it'; and immediately he will send it back here"* (Mark 11:3).

Knowing Jesus doesn't just say anything without reason, the disciples immediately went to the village opposite from where they were. No one knew how long the colt had bene there, but there was a house with a colt tied to it. When the disciples untied the colt, people standing by asked them, "What are you doing untying the colt?"

When the disciples told them exactly what the Lord had told them to say, they gave them permission. As soon as they returned with the colt, the disciples took off their coats and laid them on the donkey (Matthew chapter 21; Mark chapter 11). Jesus rode on the donkey to the top of the Mount of Olives. From there, the entire region of Jerusalem could be seen at one glance. Stopping for a moment, Jesus looked on at the Temple of Jerusalem and felt heartbroken. He knew that someday the Temple of Jerusalem would be destroyed. He couldn't help but grieve.

"For the days will come upon you when your enemies will

throw up a barricade against you, and surround you and hem you in on every side, and they will level you to the ground and your children within you, and they will not leave in you one stone upon another, because you did not recognize the time of your visitation" (Luke 19:43-44). Jesus Himself was going to be nailed upon the cross according to God's providence, but when He thought about the suffering that the people of Israel would go through after nailing Him to the cross, it was probably hard for Him to take another step.

In Jerusalem, as Passover drew near, the city was crowded with people. When the news about Jesus coming to Jerusalem spread, people began gathering in the streets. Each person holding a branch from a palm tree—some running, some following—the people cheered enthusiastically. Some people laid either their coats or their branches on the road for Jesus. "Hosanna! Blessed is He who comes in the name of the Lord, even the King of Israel."

A palm tree is a symbol for victory, and 'hosanna' means "Save us! Please!" The people believed that Jesus was their Messiah, the King who would free them from Roman oppression and bring them freedom and peace. But Jesus was not a simple political figure, or king who came to free Israel.

Jesus was the Savior of the world who would die on the cross for the sins of mankind and resurrect by destroying the power of death. As the holy and royal Son of God, He would go to sit on the right hand of the Father God. So why did such an important person enter Jerusalem riding on a young donkey?

The Fulfillment of Zechariah's Prophecy

"'Fear not, daughter of Zion; behold, your King is coming, seated on a donkey's colt.' These things His disciples did not understand at the first; but when Jesus was glorified, then they remembered that these things were written of Him, and that they had done these things to Him." (12:15-16).

Jesus was the King of kings, the Savior of the world, the Lord of all creation, but He came into Jerusalem riding on a shabby, young donkey. This was in order to fulfill the prophecy of Zechariah:

"Rejoice greatly, O daughter of Zion!
Shout in triumph, O daughter of Jerusalem!
Behold, your king is coming to you;
He is just and endowed with salvation,
Humble, and mounted on a donkey,
Even on a colt, the foal of a donkey" (Zechariah 9:9).

A young donkey that had been recently born, which no one had ever ridden before, symbolizes purity. Jesus, the Son of God who came into this world and became the firstfruits of resurrection was a holy and pure person. Therefore what He rode on had to be clean and pure.

A young colt also symbolizes humility. Jesus was by far, worthy of receiving the highest praise and honor than anyone else in the world, but just as a donkey carries the heavy burden of people's baggage, Jesus had to carry the burden of mankind's sins and die on the cross. That is why He humbly fulfilled God's Word that was prophesied in the Old Testament.

'Zion' signifies Jerusalem, which David designated as the capital. It also stands for all of Israel, or the place where God dwells. Along the same lines, 'daughter of Zion' signifies the people who believe in God, or God's children. And 'your king' signifies Jesus, God's Son.

'Fear not, daughter of Zion' tells us that we should not fear, because Jesus will enter into Jerusalem riding on a colt in order to fulfill God's plan of salvation. Originally, mankind had to shiver with fear, because from the moment we became subjects of the enemy devil and Satan's power through our sin, we could not be saved from eternal death—Hell. But with Jesus taking up the cross, the way to salvation was opened; so anyone who believes and comes before God has nothing to fear.

At that time, the disciples did not know why Jesus rode on a colt, and why the people were shaking the palm branches and shouting "Hosanna!" as they welcomed Jesus. It was after Jesus resurrected, that they realized why all these things happened, and that the prophecy of Zechariah was really about Jesus.

The Pharisees Become Anxious at the People's Welcome

"So the people, who were with Him when He called Lazarus out of the tomb and raised him from the dead, continued to testify about Him. For this reason also the people went and met Him, because they heard that

He had performed this sign. So the Pharisees said to one another, 'You see that you are not doing any good; look, the world has gone after Him'" (12:17-19).

When Jesus raised Lazarus from the dead, many Jews were there with Him. Those people told others exactly what they saw with their eyes. The news about this event spread so rapidly and made such a big impact that there was no one in the region who did not know about it. Everyone who heard the news—about how a man was brought back to life after being dead for four days—wanted to see Jesus. So when the people found out that this Jesus was coming to Jerusalem, what do you think happened? People poured into the streets, and shouts of acclamation and cheering filled the air.

But there were those who looked on at this scene with disturbed glances and nervous stares. Those were the high priests and Pharisees. They were worried that their power and authority may be taken from them, and they began to fear that their plan to kill Jesus may not be as easy as they had thought. They said to one another, "You see that you are not doing any good; look, the world has gone after Him."

There was evidence that God was with Jesus, and many people were following Him. This should have been enough to cause the Pharisees to realize that their judgment was wrong and change their ways. But for some reason, though they certainly had eyes to see and ears to hear, they acted and spoke as though they were blind and deaf. This was because there was no truth in their hearts. But the sad part about this is that they were not Gentiles who didn't know the truth—they were leaders and teachers who claimed to worship God with more zeal than anyone else. They were the leaders who should have led their people to salvation; but they were the very ones who did not recognize Jesus and were going to the way opposite of salvation and toward condemnation.

The Greeks Who Wanted to See Jesus

"Now there were some Greeks among those who were going up to worship at the feast; these then came to Philip, who was from Bethsaida of Galilee, and began to ask him, saying, 'Sir, we wish to see Jesus.' Philip came and told Andrew; Andrew and Philip came and told Jesus. And Jesus answered them, saying, 'The hour has come for the Son of Man to be glorified'" (12:20-23).

Among those who came to Jerusalem to celebrate the Passover were Greeks. Some of these Greeks came to Phillip, one of Jesus' disciples. "Sir, we wish to see Jesus."

Phillip told Andrew about this, and the two went and told Jesus. Upon hearing that the Greeks want to see Him, Jesus tells them a very meaningful message, "The hour has come for the Son of Man to be glorified."

The Greeks are not simply foreigners. They signify "The spiritual thirst that comes because the hour is near" (Amos 8:11-13). Jesus taught God's words for three years. During those times, all the people who heard His words were thankful and joyful like barren land that received nourishing rain.

The closer it came to "The hour for the Son of Man to be glorified", the more spiritually thirsty the people became—those people who loved and sought after the truth. Of course they did not know that Jesus would soon be dying on the cross, but it was as though they sensed it, and wanted to see Him one more time, and listen to His words one more time.

The Parable of the One Grain of Wheat

"Truly, truly, I say to you, unless a grain of wheat falls into the earth and dies, it remains alone; but if it dies, it bears much fruit. He who loves his life loses it, and he who hates his life in this world will keep it to life eternal. If anyone serves Me, he must follow Me; and where I am, there My servant will be also; if anyone serves Me, the Father will honor him" (12:24-26).

Speaking about where He needed to go, Jesus told the people a parable about the single grain of wheat, while prophesying about His death and resurrection. If you sow one grain of wheat, you can gain about 50-100 fruits from it. But if you don't sow it, no matter how much you wait, you gain nothing.

Jesus humbled Himself and submitted to God to the point of dying on the cross. This process of completing the way of the cross was necessary to lead the sinners from death to life. The result? Anyone who accepts Jesus as his Savior is forgiven of his sins and receives eternal life. As Jesus said, "If one grain of wheat falls into the earth and dies, it bears much fruit," when

Jesus, the only begotten Son, died on the cross, many children of God could then be gained as fruit.

Jesus also said, "He who loves his life loses it, and he who hates his life in this world will keep it to life eternal." 'His Life' doesn't just mean a person's life. It also stands for whatever one treasures as dearly as his life. Money, fame, power, knowledge, children, self-esteem can be such things. Anyone who loves these things as much as his own life ultimately loses them all. But if people cast off these fleshly things from their hearts, they can gain the things that are eternal.

After meeting the Lord, all the worldly things the apostle Paul had once cherished he considered as rubbish (Philippians 3:8). He knew that the knowledge of Christ Jesus was the most valuable treasure in the world. As a result, he became a child of God who sought after the truth and received God's guidance. As Jesus said anyone who hates his life will keep it to life eternal, Paul was raised to a position of glory as bright as the sun in Heaven. So when a person serves Jesus, God honors him (John 12:26).

Jesus' Prayer

"'Now My soul has become troubled; and what shall I say, "Father, save Me from this hour"? But for this purpose I came to this hour. Father, glorify Your name.' Then a voice came out of heaven: 'I have both glorified it, and will glorify it again.' So the crowd of people who stood by and heard it were saying that it had thundered; others were saying, 'An angel has spoken to Him.' Jesus answered and said, 'This voice has not come for My sake, but for your sakes'" (12:27-30).

In a little while, the spotless one and one without blemish, Jesus, the holy one, had to take up all the sins of mankind and receive the same punishment as that of a vicious criminal. So Jesus makes this confession to God: "Now My soul has become troubled; and what shall I say, 'Father, save Me from this hour'?"

From this confession, we can see Jesus' human nature. But when He said "Save Me from this hour," He was not saying He didn't want to take up the cross—He said this to show how heavy the burden of sin was, which He had to carry.

"But for this purpose I came to this hour. Father, glorify Your name." Through this statement we can see Jesus' divine nature. When He confessed that He wanted to glorify God by completing His purpose for coming into this world, a voice came out of heaven: "I have both glorified it, and will glorify it again."

This conversation shows us how much God loves Jesus. God was saying that He had already been glorified through Jesus, and that He would be glorified again after Jesus' death on the cross, and His resurrection thereafter.

When a loud voice came from heaven during Jesus' prayer, people said either that it had thundered, or an angel had spoken to Him. At that time, Jesus said the voice did not come for *His* sake, but "for your sakes." The reason being, God, who is basically one with Jesus, had no need to answer in a loud voice, but He did this to plant faith into the people who were standing by.

Jesus came to this world to fulfill God's will. This will was to save mankind, give them true life, and to let them recover their true image, which was once created in the image of God. There were times when He was hungry and thirsty, but He did His best to spread God's will and the gospel and give life to as many people as possible.

Jesus Tells About His Death on the Cross

"'Now judgment is upon this world; now the ruler of this world will be cast out. And I, if I am lifted up from the earth, will draw all men to Myself.' But He was saying this to indicate the kind of death by which He was to die. The crowd then answered Him, 'We have heard out of the Law that the Christ is to remain forever; and how can You say, "The Son of Man must be lifted up"? Who is this Son of Man?'" (12:31-34)

"Ruler of this world" refers to the enemy devil and Satan, who is the ruler of this world. In this world, there are laws which people need to abide by. When people do not abide by them, they receive a punishment. In the same way, in the spiritual world, if one sins, he faces the penalty of death (Romans 6:23). The enemy devil and Satan came to break the spiritual law because he killed Jesus, who had no sin. So the enemy devil and Satan became a lawbreaker. This is what Jesus meant when He said, "judgment is upon this world."

Jesus could not be bound by death because He was sinless. Therefore God released Him from the torment of death, and raised Him back to life. And because Jesus destroyed the power of death, now anyone who receives Jesus Christ is no longer subject to Satan's oppression. As a result of breaking the spiritual law, the enemy devil and Satan were cast out, and mankind, who were once sinners, are now called righteous, and can reign in life through Jesus Christ (Romans 5:17).

"I, if I am lifted up from the earth, will draw all men to Myself." When Jesus said this, He was saying that by taking up all the sins and dying on the cross, He was leading people from the dark to the light; and from death to life. This is possible because though Jesus had to die, He would resurrect, and through this event, many people will come to believe that Jesus is the Christ, and go to Heaven. Jesus knew how He was going to die. Jesus knew very well about the providence of the cross, the secret which was hidden since before the ages. That is why He talked about His death upon the cross ahead of time, and then completely fulfilled His mission.

"We have heard out of the Law that the Christ is to remain forever; and how can You say, 'The Son of Man must be lifted up'? Who is this Son of Man?" The people who neither knew what was to come, nor understood the spiritual meaning of Jesus' words became confused with many thoughts.

"The Law" signifies the Pentateuch, or the five books of Moses—Genesis, Exodus, Leviticus, Numbers, and Deuteronomy. The people said they heard of the Law that "Christ is to remain forever." But to be exact, this information is not found in the Pentateuch. It is actually found in the prophecies of the Old Testament.

In Isaiah 9:7 it says, *"There will be no end to the increase of His government or of peace, on the throne of David and over his kingdom, to establish it and to uphold it with justice and righteousness from then on and forevermore the zeal of the LORD of hosts will accomplish this."* And in Daniel 7:14 it reads, *"And to Him was given dominion, glory and a kingdom, that all the peoples, nations and men of every language might serve Him. His dominion is an everlasting dominion which will not pass away; and His kingdom is one which will not be destroyed."*

At that time, the Law, to which the people referred, was very different from its original form. The Pharisees and Sadducees labeled even the most trivial things into laws, and at times they interpreted the Law or changed the Law for their own benefit. That is why even after witnessing all the miraculous things Jesus was doing, they did not understand. They also did not understand the prophecies from the Old Testament regarding the Christ. They interpreted God's will within the boundaries of limited human thought. However, with certainty, as prophesied in the Old Testament, Jesus Christ remains forever and His power is unchanging.

Jesus Leaves the People and Hides

"So Jesus said to them, 'For a little while longer the Light is among you. Walk while you have the Light, so that darkness will not overtake you; he who walks in the darkness does not know where he goes. While you have the Light, believe in the Light, so that you may

become sons of Light. These things Jesus spoke, and He went away and hid Himself from them" (12:35-36).

The "Light" here signifies Jesus (Romans 9:5). As the Light, Jesus helped people realize their true identity, and He gave them direction in life: In everything that you do—whether you eat or drink—do it all to the glory of God. As long as one stays in Christ, he does not wander any more, and he can gain the solution to all of life's problems.

But when Jesus talked about dying on the cross, even the people who believed that Jesus was the Messiah were shaken in their faith. So to keep their faith from being shaken, Jesus told them that His death on the cross was not something that would occur right away.

He told them since there was still some time left, they should truly believe in Him, and walk in the Light. And even when the darkness seems more powerful, He warned them not to be overtaken by it. What He meant was even though He dies on the cross, do not think it is the end and do not lose hope.

Seeing the people's faith shaken just at hearing a little about what was to come, Jesus urged them again, "Believe in the Light, so that you may become sons of Light." This meant that if they believed in Jesus, through them, God would show that He is alive, and make each of them the light of the world. After saying this, Jesus left them and hid. He did this to quietly avoid those people who could not understand His spiritual words and who were once again doubting and not believing.

The Teaching of the Messiah

Right before the Passover, Jesus entered Jerusalem humbly riding on a colt. Many people welcomed Him and followed Him. But that was only for a short while. Among the people who heard Jesus' words, some became shaken in their faith and began to doubt. But the fact that the people wouldn't believe that He was the Messiah, even though He performed so many signs, was already prophesied by the prophet Isaiah.

Isaiah's Prophecy about the Messiah

"But though He had performed so many signs before them, yet they were not believing in Him. This was to fulfill the word of Isaiah the prophet which he spoke:

'Lord, who has believed our report? And to whom has the arm of the Lord been revealed?'" (12:37-38).

The prophet Isaiah served as a prophet from the 10th king, King Uzziah to the 13th king, King Hezekiah. He prophesied about the Messiah's arrival under dismal circumstances of the time, the recovery of Israel, and a blessed future (Isaiah 60:14, 20). He prophesied in detail about the appearance of Jesus, the coming Messiah, His suffering, and the outcome. He also told about how so many people would not accept and believe in Jesus who comes as the Messiah, and that they would reject Him.

"Who has believed our message? And to whom has the arm of the LORD been revealed?" (Isaiah 53:1) In this passage we can feel Isaiah's frustration and sorrow for the people's lack of faith. When we hold onto the gospel and accept Jesus as our Savior, God forgives our sins and brings us from death to life, and we gain salvation. But why is there such a small number of people enabled by God's power and who are saved?

The Reason People Could Not Believe in Jesus as the Messiah

"For this reason they could not believe, for Isaiah said again, 'He has blinded their eyes and He hardened their heart, so that they would not see with their eyes and perceive with their heart, and be converted and I heal them.' These things Isaiah said because he saw His glory, and he spoke of Him" (12:39-41).

Isaiah knew the reason why people could not believe in Jesus. The reason was that "He has blinded their eyes and He hardened their heart, so that they would not see with their eyes and perceive with their heart." What does this mean? God does not make some people good and some people evil. All people have evil at the root of their hearts. But when they don't cast out this evil and continue acting upon it, in the end, they ultimately become blinded to the truth that is the light.

For example, if a haughty person does not cast out his pride, and continues to judge and condemn other people, he is piling evil over evil. Therefore his heart will become more calloused, and ultimately, he will go to the way of death. If we look around, we see people who know smoking and drinking is bad for their health, and yet they continue to smoke and drink. Then we see them suffering from all kinds of illnesses, or become alcoholics and lead miserable lives. This is the result of continuing to indulge in something even though they know it is bad.

Likewise, the people who rejected Jesus could not accept Jesus because of the evil in their hearts, not because God made them that way. Then why does the Scripture make it sound like God covered their eyes and hardened their hearts? This is because God has nothing to do with people who intentionally abandon His Law and have already become slaves to the enemy devil and Satan, and who continue to act with evil. God leaves these kinds of people alone. Therefore, without God's intervention, their eyes become covered and their hearts become calloused, all on their own.

However, when *His* children sin, God does not leave them alone. He leads them so they turn from their evil ways. If, for example, a believer with faith does not keep the Lord's day holy or does not give their tithes, or does something that does not please God, God will allow trials and tribulations to come to them, according to the seriousness of the sin. Drawing this kind of boundary, God is constantly sending a sign to His children to turn away from sin.

In the aforementioned verse it states, "He has blinded their eyes and He hardened their heart, so that they would not see with their eyes and perceive with their heart, and be converted and I heal them." First, we see with 'the eyes', God's words and His works and gain faith. And when we 'perceive with the heart', we are not only listening to God's Word, but we are becoming enlightened, and turning away from evil.

When we perceive with the heart, we transform into beautiful people of truth. We know that this is the sole way to eternal life. So when we see with our eyes and perceive with our hearts and turn away from evil, God will heal us, and answer our prayers. But because people do not cast away their evil, their eyes become blinded, and their hearts become hardened, and they cannot receive healing.

The prophet Isaiah lived about 700 years before Jesus came, but he saw the Lord's glory and spoke out about the Lord. This was because he had a good heart, and he thoroughly received God's love. He was completely different from the high priest and the Pharisees who couldn't even recognize Jesus when He was standing right before their eyes.

"Nevertheless many even of the rulers believed in Him, but because of the Pharisees they were not confessing Him, for fear that they would be put out of the synagogue; for they loved the approval of men rather than the approval of God" (12:42-43).

'Rulers' refer to people who are paid by the king's palace, army, or country. They are also the people who work or serve in the temple. Leaders of the Council, temple, palace, court, or people who serve the king in the inner courts, are all considered 'rulers'. Even among these types of rulers of society, the number of people who believed in Jesus Christ grew.

But out of fear of being put out of the synagogue, they could not reveal their faith. If they confessed Jesus as Christ, they would not only be deprived of their social status, but they would also have to put up with the people's persecution and ridicule. So even if they had faith, they did not have perfect faith, or a sincere heart (Hebrews 10:22). They loved the glory of men, the riches, fame, and powers of this world more than the glory of God.

"I Have Come to Save the World"

"And Jesus cried out and said, 'He who believes in Me, does not believe in Me but in Him who sent Me. He who sees Me sees the One who sent Me. I have come as Light into the world, so that everyone who believes in Me will not remain in darkness. If anyone hears My sayings and does not keep them, I do not judge him; for I did not come to judge the world, but to save the world'" (12:44-47).

Special courtesy is shown to diplomatic envoys that are sent from a certain country as its representatives. It is because dealing with the envoy is like dealing with the country that sent them, or the highest leader of that country. In the same way, if a person believes in God, he will trust and obey the prophet who is sent by God. Furthermore, who is Jesus? He is God's Son, who came to this world and showed many signs. Even though we cannot see God with our eyes, through the miraculous signs that Jesus performed, God made sure we could believe in Him.

Jesus came to this world as the true Light. If we are stumbling around in pitch darkness, and we come across one single ray of light, that light will be most precious. Likewise, while we were in the darkness of sin, and we did not know which way to go, Jesus came as the Light and became the way, the truth, and the life for us. So no matter what problems we may have, if we pray to the Father God in the name of 'Jesus Christ', who is the Light, we can receive the key to resolve any problem.

Therefore it is only right that we believe in and obey Jesus, the Son of God, who came into this world in the flesh. But there are so many people who do not believe in Jesus or obey Him.

Jesus did not come to condemn the world. This is why He said, 'Even though man does not keep My word, I do not condemn him.' This means that not only Jesus, but God also, is not quick to scorn and reprove when a person does something wrong.

Rather, He waits patiently and helps the person realize His will, and thereby come to know Him and seek Him. And to those who love Him, He will meet them and shed His grace upon them. Of course He teaches about the judgment and punishment after that; but He leads us to the way of salvation with joy and thanksgiving, rather than fear. This is why Jesus said, "I did not come to judge the world, but to save the world."

The Final Judgment and Eternal Life

"He who rejects Me and does not receive My sayings, has one who judges him; the word I spoke is what will judge him at the last day. For I did not speak on My own initiative, but the Father Himself who sent Me has given Me a commandment as to what to say and what to speak. I know that His commandment is eternal life; therefore the things I speak, I speak just as the Father has told Me" (12:48-50).

2 Peter 3:9 states, *"The Lord is not slow about His promise, as some count slowness, but is patient toward you, not wishing for any to perish but for all to come to repentance."* And in 1 Timothy 2:4, it says, *"[God] desires all men to be saved and to come to the knowledge of the truth."*

Like this, God leads each person to the way of salvation, each according to their measure of faith, so no one feels burdened or feels burnt-out in the process. Still, there are so many people who turn away from Him and go the way of death, which is very tragic. Regarding this, Jesus said, "He who rejects Me and does not receive My sayings, has one who judges him; the word I spoke is what will judge him at the last day."

God wants everyone to receive salvation, and in order to fulfill His will, Jesus taught God's Word while being here on earth, and through complete sacrifice, He completed the way of salvation. So as it is written in Romans 10:13, *"Whoever will call on the name of the Lord will be saved,"* the doorway to salvation was made wide open.

However, to those who do not believe in the Lord, a severe judgment awaits them on the last day. God made His eternal power and divine nature to be clearly evident in His creation, so that everyone will be without excuse in front of the judgment seat (Romans 1:19-20). On that day, no one will be able to say, "I never heard about God. I don't know who Jesus Christ is. I don't know about the way of salvation."

Hebrews 9:27 says, *"And inasmuch as it is appointed for men to die once and after this comes judgment."* While we are living in this world, God will lead us in many different ways so that we can receive salvation and become likened in His image. But we must remember that in the last day judgment awaits us. Children of God will receive eternal life, and receive heavenly rewards according to the actions we sowed while here on earth. However, those who do not believe in God will have to ultimately fall into Hell and receive the eternal punishment.

Jesus never did one thing according to His own will. He did

all things according to God's will, and according to His time. Even with every word He spoke, He spoke with a clear purpose. That is why even now, He boldly lets us know that the words He spoke were God's commands.

"For I did not speak on My own initiative, but the Father Himself who sent Me has given Me a commandment as to what to say and what to speak. I know that His commandment is eternal life; therefore the things I speak, I speak just as the Father has told Me."

The reason God showed His power through all the signs and wonders that Jesus performed, and the reason He resurrected Jesus three days after He died on the cross, was to free mankind from sin and give them eternal life. Jesus knew this will of God the Father better than anyone else. This is why Jesus obeyed Him completely, without a fraction of a mistake. Like this, if we obey God in everything we do, we can also fulfill His will completely.

Chapter 13

The Last Passover Supper

Jesus Washes the Disciples' Feet

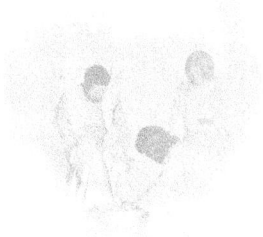

Oftentimes we are moved in our hearts when we hear a beautiful love story where people show sacrificial love for one another. Once in a while when we hear a story about parents who sacrificed their own life for their child, tears fill our eyes. But this kind of love cannot even begin to compare to God's love for us. It is written in Isaiah 49:15, *"Can a woman forget her nursing child and have no compassion on the son of her womb? Even these may forget, but I will not forget you."* Jesus, who came to this world with God's heart showed this same love to us. This love was the love that made Him take up the cross for all mankind.

Jesus' Heart: The Love That Loves to the Bitter End

"Now before the Feast of the Passover, Jesus knowing that His hour had come that He would depart out of this world to the Father, having loved His own who were in the world, He loved them to the end. During supper, the devil having already put into the heart of Judas Iscariot, the son of Simon, to betray Him..." (13:1-2).

When the Scripture says "His hour had come that He would depart out of this world to the Father", it means that the time had come for Jesus to die on the cross. But even though He knew His time of suffering was coming near, He loved His people to the end. Until the very last moment, Jesus taught with the truth—even Judas Iscariot, who Jesus knew would betray Him.

This was after Judas Iscariot had already made the decision to betray Jesus. Calmly and deliberately, he mingled with the other disciples very naturally, but after the incident with Mary and the perfume, he schemed to sell his teacher to the high priests and sought only for the opportune time. After becoming a disciple, the other disciples did whatever they could to try to understand Jesus' teachings and follow in His footsteps. To the contrary, even while witnessing God's power, Judas continued to give in to his doubts and complaints. Not only did he refuse to cast out the evil in his heart, he continued to pile up evil with his fleshly thoughts.

Some of the fleshly thoughts are hate, envy, jealousy,

arrogance, judgment, and condemnation. Fleshly thoughts are all thoughts that are not of truth. When a person's heart is evil, he can only have fleshly thoughts as the enemy Satan controls his evil heart. As it is written in Romans 8:7, *"Because the mind set on the flesh is hostile toward God; for it does not subject itself to the law of God, for it is not even able to do so,"* Judas Iscariot was filled with fleshly thoughts and ultimately, he ended up committing a grave and unwashable sin.

What we need to be cautious of is this: anyone who is filled with evil in his heart can become subject to the enemy Satan's control, just like Judas Iscariot. If we don't want to be controlled by the enemy Satan, we need to transform our hearts so it is filled with the truth. And, with the help of the Holy Spirit, we need to guard our hearts with good thoughts, and thoughts of truth. To do this, we need to rejoice always, pray without ceasing, and in everything give thanks. The enemy Satan cannot creep up to those who live like this.

The Last Passover Supper

"Jesus, knowing that the Father had given all things into His hands, and that He had come forth from God and was going back to God…" (13:3)

On Thursday afternoon, the day before He was captured, Jesus prepared for the Passover meal, in order to spend His last night with the disciples. The process of preparing for the

Passover is depicted more clearly in Luke chapter 22, rather than the Gospel of John. Jesus called Peter and John and gave them a special task: *"Go and prepare the Passover for us, so that we may eat it"* (v. 8).

When the disciples asked where to prepare the meal, Jesus told them to go into the city and follow a man carrying a pitcher of water into a house and tell the owner of the house what Jesus said. He even explained exactly how the owner would react. Peter and John immediately went into the city. And lo and behold, there was the man carrying a pitcher of water! So they followed the man into a house and spoke to the owner of the house. *"The Teacher says to you, 'Where is the guest room in which I may eat the Passover with My disciples?'"* (v. 11)

The owner, as if he was waiting for Peter and John, led them to a large upper room. When the Passover meal was prepared, Jesus took the twelve disciples and sat with them in the upper room. At that time as He was looking at them, His heart was filled with more love for them than ever before. Knowing that He had to leave them—according to God's will—when the night is over, how sad He must have felt, thinking about the disciples who would be left behind!

"The Father had given all things into His hands" refers to the mission that God bestowed upon Jesus. This was the mission of saving all mankind. In the Old Testament times, when a person sinned, he had to sacrifice a cow, sheep, goat, or dove in order to be forgiven by God. This was according to the law of sacrifice which reads that without the shedding of blood, there is no forgiveness of sins (Hebrews 9:22). This is also the reason Jesus had to die on the cross and shed His blood to save mankind from their sins. The Scripture also states that Jesus knew that "He had come forth from God and was going back to God," which means He knew that He would soon shed His blood on the cross and die.

Jesus Washes the Disciples' Feet

"...got up from supper, and laid aside His garments; and taking a towel, He girded Himself. Then He poured water into the basin, and began to wash the

:: Jesus washing Peter's feet (mosaic on the exterior of St. Peter's Basilica)

disciples' feet and to wipe them with the towel with which He was girded" (13:4-5).

That night in the upper room, Jesus got up from His last supper and put aside His outer garments and put a towel around His waist. Then He poured water into a basin and washed and wiped the disciples' feet as they watched in silence.

To the Jews who lived in a region known for its barren and dusty ground, there was a custom of washing a guest's feet; but this was usually done by a servant. But Jesus, who was their teacher, was washing their feet, so how surprised and embarrassed the disciples must have been! Not knowing how to stop Him, they probably didn't know what to do at that moment.

The reason Jesus washed the disciples' feet was to teach them what kind of attitude and heart they needed to have when they took on the important mission of spreading the gospel and witnessing about the Lord's resurrection. Jesus wanted to make sure they understood and realized God's will and understood God's love. He wanted them to know that they had to do all things with a sacrificing and heart of serving when they began sharing the gospel.

Jesus' Conversation with Simon Peter

"So He came to Simon Peter. He said to Him, 'Lord, do You wash my feet?' Jesus answered and said to him, 'What I do you do not realize now, but you will understand hereafter.' Peter said to Him, 'Never shall You wash my feet!' Jesus answered him, 'If I do not wash you, you have no part with Me'" (13:6-8).

When Jesus came to Simon Peter and tried to wash his feet, he asked in a bashful way, "Lord, do You wash my feet?" Jesus answered, "What I do you do not realize now, but you will understand hereafter."

According to the customs and rules he was aware of, it was just not right for a teacher to wash the feet of his disciple. If Peter had completely trusted Jesus, he probably would have thought that there was some special reason Jesus was doing what He did. But because what he saw did not concur well with his own knowledge and thoughts, he refused to have his feet washed by Jesus. This was the result of Peter still depending on his fleshly thoughts. "Never shall You wash my feet!"

Jesus knew that when the disciples share the gospel with the heart of a servant, many people will come to have true faith. He also knew that only when they become apostles who serve, would they be considered great in Heaven. When Jesus humbled Himself and submitted to God's will to the point of death, God raised Him up high above all things. Jesus washed the disciples' feet in order to give them this spiritual teaching, but Peter declined thinking his thoughts were more correct. Seeing Peter getting in the way of fulfilling God's will, Jesus continued to speak to him, "If I do not wash you, you have no part with Me."

The feet can be considered the dirtiest part of the human body, especially in those days. At that time people did not have good shoes like we have today. The people wore sandals tied with leather strings, so the feet were always covered with sand and dust. So washing dirty feet not only symbolized "The model of servant-hood", but it also carried a greater significance of Jesus "Washing away the dirty sins of man."

As it is written in the Scripture, *"For out of the heart come evil thoughts, murders, adulteries, fornications, thefts, false witness, slanders. These are the things which defile the man; but to eat with unwashed hands does not defile the man"* (Matthew 15:19-20), Jesus wanted the disciples to realize that they needed to cast out their sins and wash themselves of sin. Water symbolizes God's Word. Only when a person washes his sins with God's Word can he serve with his heart, and only then can he be called a son of God.

If a person claims to believe in God but does not wash himself of sin, he cannot meet God, and he has nothing to do with God. Jesus, who washed the feet of His disciples, wanted them to wash their heart of sin and become true children of God.

> "Simon Peter said to Him, 'Lord, then wash not only my feet, but also my hands and my head.' Jesus said to him, 'He who has bathed needs only to wash his feet, but is completely clean; and you are clean, but not all of you.' For He knew the one who was betraying Him; for this reason He said, 'Not all of you are clean.'" (13:9-11)

Upon hearing that he won't have anything to do with Jesus

unless Jesus washes his feet, Peter quickly replied, "Lord, then wash not only my feet, but also my hands and my head."

Just a moment ago, Peter told Jesus He should never wash his feet, but now he was telling Jesus to wash not only his feet, but his hands and his head as well. Once again, we can see Peter's honesty—never hiding what's in his heart—and outgoing personality—always wanting to be in the center of the action. This kind of nature often earned Peter some scolding, but even then, Jesus saw Peter's potential to change and taught him another lesson. "He who has bathed needs only to wash his feet."

When Jesus talked about "He who has already bathed," He is talking about "He who already has faith." This is referring to someone who has become a believer from hearing God's words and seeing signs and wonders. So when a believer needs to have his feet washed, it means that until he gains complete faith, he should always look inside of himself and meditate on God's Word and become transformed into a person of truth. If we claim to have faith and love God, and yet we don't cast out evil from our hearts, it means nothing. We cannot share grace with others; nor can we lead others to the way of truth. Therefore it is important to cast out all evil from our hearts and become transformed by God's Word.

Then if the disciples at the time were in a state where they hadn't cast out all of their sins, why did Jesus say, "You are clean"? When Jesus said they were clean, He meant that they were spiritually awake. Whenever they listened to God's Word, they tried to figure out the spiritual significance of His Word, and they were making every effort to keep themselves in check and to have complete, wholesome faith.

These kinds of people are acknowledged as being clean, even though they may not have cast off their sins completely, because they are doing their best to become wholesome, with faith. But one person, Judas Iscariot, was not like that. He thought no one knew that he had visited the high priests, but Jesus already knew. As darkness is uncovered in the presence of the light, Jesus even knew what was inside of Judas' heart. So in order to help him come to a realization, He said, "You are clean, but not all of you." Jesus wanted to give Judas one last chance to change.

A Lesson about Love and Humility

"So when He had washed their feet, and taken His garments and reclined at the table again, He said to them, 'Do you know what I have done to you? You call Me Teacher and Lord; and you are right, for so I am. If I then, the Lord and the Teacher, washed your feet, you also ought to wash one another's feet'" (13:12-14).

After washing the disciples' feet, Jesus put His garments back on and reclined at the table again. He looked around at the disciples. "Do you know what I have done to you?" He added, "You also ought to wash one another's feet."

Even though Jesus Himself had to leave, for the disciples He was leaving behind in this world and for those who would be spreading the gospel, He wanted them to maintain a beautiful relationship with one another by serving, loving, and comforting one another. But this message doesn't just pertain to the disciples. All people who believe in God are brothers and sisters of one family in Christ; therefore we must edify each other and lead one another in love.

In 2 Peter 1:7, it says to supply *"in your godliness, brotherly kindness, and in your brotherly kindness, love."* And in Romans 12:10, it says, *"Be devoted to one another in brotherly love; give preference to one another in honor…"*

But Jesus did not just say, "Serve and love one another." He said, "If I then, the Lord and the Teacher, washed your feet, you also ought to wash one another's feet."

This means that a person who is the head, a person who is in a teaching position must serve, give, and sacrifice first, in order to lead others to the truth. Believers in the Lord who are forerunners of faith must model after Jesus through sacrifice and service. And in order to fulfill our calling well, we must confess from the center of our hearts that we are what we are because of God's grace, and we must consider others better than ourselves.

The Parable of the Slave and the Master

"For I gave you an example that you also should do as I did to you. Truly, truly, I say to you, a slave is not greater than his master, nor is one who is sent greater than the one who sent him. If you know these things, you are blessed if you do them" (13:15-17).

If someone lives an unrighteous life and he teaches another person to live a righteous life, would his teaching be effective? This is the same for the truth. If we do not live according to God's Word, and we try to teach other people, we can never change them. On the contrary, if we live according to the truth and teach others to do the same, then God guarantees our words; therefore the people whom we teach will undergo change.

Titus 2:7-8 says, *"In all things show yourself to be an example of good deeds, with purity in doctrine, dignified, sound in speech which is beyond reproach, so that the opponent will be put to shame, having nothing bad to say about us."* The enemy devil and Satan cannot disturb anyone who is leading a model life at all times through good actions. They are successful in everything that they do, and their walk in life is straight. Because it is so important to be a good example in their actions, Jesus washed the feet of His disciples and showed them the model of serving.

And using the illustration of "the master and the slave" and "the one who sent and the one that is sent", Jesus taught the relationship between God and Jesus. The "master" and the "one who sent" signify God, and the "slave" and the "one who was sent" signify Jesus Himself. Philippians 2:7 calls Jesus a bond-servant who was made in the likeness of men, and in John 17:18, Jesus says God sent Him into this world.

In whatever He did, Jesus acknowledged God at all times; and He knew clearly God's heart and will in completing the way of salvation for mankind through Him (John 3:16; Luke 5:32).

In order to fulfill the will of God, Jesus only obeyed even to the point of crucifixion (Philippians 2:8). Though He was the Son of God, all of this was not easily accomplished. Jesus always had to pray so that He could fully understand what the will of God is and how He would be able to bear proper fruits in accordance with His will. Thus, His accomplishing everything in accordance with God's will gives us the perfect example.

This Jesus, who showed love and humility in His actions, reminded His disciples, "Truly, truly, I say to you, a slave is not greater than his master, nor is one who is sent greater than the one who sent him. If you know these things, you are blessed if you do them." What Jesus meant here is that God's blessings will be upon those who always fear God who is the master of all the souls. And, God's blessing will be with those who always seek God's will and try to act accordingly, wherever they may be.

The Prophecy about Judas Iscariot's Betrayal

"I do not speak of all of you. I know the ones I have chosen; but it is that the Scripture may be fulfilled, 'He who eats My bread has lifted up his heel against Me.' From now on I am telling you before it comes to pass, so that when it does occur, you may believe that I am He" (13:18-19).

No matter how much a parent teaches his child to go the best way, if that child has no will of his own, he cannot go that way. This is similar to Jesus teaching which way is the way to blessing. But, Judas Iscariot ultimately betrayed Jesus anyway. This event was actually prophesied a long time ago. Jesus referred to Psalm 41:9, which states, *"Even my close friend in whom I trusted, who ate my bread, has lifted up his heel against me."* In saying this Jesus told the disciples that one of them would betray Him.

"He who eats my bread" refers to someone who always abides with Jesus, and who learns God's Word, which is the bread of life. And when Jesus used the phrase "has lifted up his heel against me" it means that someone who had been walking in the same direction with Him has changed his direction, meaning he has gone away from Jesus and is now going a different way. He was talking about Judas Iscariot, who would betray Jesus and sell Him over to the Jews. Now there was a reason Jesus told the disciples about this before it happened. "So that when it does occur, you may believe that I am He." Jesus wanted to warn the disciples so that when He is captured, they do not become shocked or scared, but rather realize, "Oh, God's will is being accomplished," and prepare for what is to come.

Jesus, who Is One With God

"Truly, truly, I say to you, he who receives whomever I send receives Me; and he who receives Me receives Him who sent Me" (13:20).

Accepting Jesus, whom God sent, is the same as accepting

God, and accepting the one that Jesus sent, is the same as accepting Jesus. The fact that the events that Jesus talked about occurred exactly the way He said they would was evidence that we can put faith in His Word. This was evidence that showed Jesus is God's Son, and that He is one with God.

In order to understand God's providence in sending His one and only Son Jesus into this world to open the way of salvation, we need to first accept Jesus. If we do not accept Jesus as Christ, we cannot understand God's providence for saving mankind. 1 John 5:12 says, *"He who has the Son has the life; he who does not have the Son of God does not have the life."* This shows that the relationship between God and Jesus is that of Father and Son.

This kind of relationship pertains to those who accept Jesus as well. In Mark 16:20, it states, *"And they went out and preached everywhere, while the Lord worked with them, and confirmed the word by the signs that followed."* Jesus was actually with the disciples in spirit. Therefore for those who believed in the disciples' words, it was the same as accepting the Lord.

"One of You Will Betray Me"

After washing the disciples' feet, Jesus taught them a lesson on love and humility, and then prophesied about Judas' betrayal. There is an old Korean saying that when one bites down on all ten fingers, there is not one finger that does not hurt. In the same way, knowing that one of His disciples, who had been with Him for so long, would betray Him, how do you think Jesus felt? How painful it must have been for Him!

"One of You Will Betray Me"

"When Jesus had said this, He became troubled in spirit, and testified and said, 'Truly, truly, I say to you, that one of you will betray Me.' The disciples began looking at one another, at a loss to know of which one He was speaking. There was reclining on Jesus' bosom one of His disciples, whom Jesus loved. So Simon Peter gestured to him, and said to him, 'Tell us who it is of whom He is speaking'" (13:21-14).

Jesus spoke these words with great difficulty. The whole time He knew that one of His disciples would sell Him over to the Jews, but this was the first time He spoke out about it. For a moment, everyone in the room began to stir with discomfort. No one expected to hear what Jesus said, so they all became a bit confused. Very soon, the disciples went from uncomfortable, to curious. "Who could He be talking about?" "Who would do such an evil thing?" Then, everyone began to glance at each other with probing eyes.

They each became a little concerned, wondering, *"Could He be talking about me?"* (Mark 14:19). Peter couldn't wait any longer, and he motioned to the disciple leaning on Jesus' bosom, telling him to ask Jesus which disciple He was talking about. But the Scripture does not mention the name of the disciple who was leaning on Jesus—it just says one of the disciples "whom Jesus loved". This disciple was actually the apostle John, the author of the Gospel of John.

John did not reveal his name in his book. Instead, he liked to use the phrase "The disciple whom Jesus loved" when speaking about himself (John 21:20). The son of Zebedee, John was the brother of James. Depending on their personality, people express their love in different ways. Like the youngest son of a family, John followed Jesus around with utmost adoration and love.

But what significance is there in the fact that while all the disciples served and followed Jesus so closely, one of them ended up selling Him? What we can learn here is that no matter how wonderful the environment may be for growing in faith, if we do not cast out evil from our hearts, we may end up with a terrible outcome.

When Jesus opened the eyes of the blind, healed the sick, and made the lame walk, Judas Iscariot was there next to Him, witnessing every event. Judas should have been able to believe that Jesus was a person of truth, and that God was with Him. But instead of having faith, Judas stole money; and dreaming of gaining great power someday, he let his selfish ambition drive him. And because he did not cast out that evil from his heart, he ultimately ended up committing an irreversible sin.

The lesson we need to learn from this is this: those who receive more special grace and love from God—like the disciples—need to be more careful to fully examine themselves at all times. The truth tells us to "serve", so we should check to see if we are "serving", and not "wanting to be served". The word tells us to "seek the benefit of others", so then we need to check if we are really always seeking the benefit of others before ourselves.

"Lord, Who Is It?"

"He, leaning back thus on Jesus' bosom, said to Him, 'Lord, who is it?' Jesus then answered, 'That is the one for whom I shall dip the morsel and give it to him.' So when He had dipped the morsel, He took and gave it to Judas, the son of Simon Iscariot. After the morsel, Satan then entered into him. Therefore Jesus said to him, 'What you do, do quickly'" (13:25-27)

John was curious too. So when Peter gestured to him to ask the Lord, he asked, "Lord, who is it?" Jesus said, "That is the one for whom I shall dip the morsel and give it to him."

Jesus dipped a morsel and handed it to Judas. Without a word, Judas took the bread from the teacher. As He looked at Judas at this time, Jesus' eyes reflected many different emotions. His eyes were filled with grief and mourning, and love. Jesus could not give up on him, but He knew that ultimately, Judas would never turn from his ways.

So why did Jesus reveal who would betray Him by dipping the morsel and then handing it to Judas? Even to the last moment, Jesus wanted to give Judas a chance to repent and turn from his ways. The same scene is found in Matthew 26:23-24: *"And He answered, 'He who dipped his hand with Me in the bowl is the one who will betray Me. The Son of Man is to go, just as it is written of Him; but woe to that man by whom the Son of Man is betrayed! It would have been good for that man if he had not been born.'"*

Judas, being pierced at the heart, asked, "Surely it is not I, Rabbi?" And Jesus answered him, "You have said it yourself." By this time, Judas should have known that Jesus knew what he was planning to do. But he still was deceitful and did not change his mind.

Another reason why Jesus dipped the morsel and handed it to Judas was for the other disciples to know. After His resurrection and ascension into heaven, as they recollected everything that happened, Jesus wanted them to realize that in order to open the door of salvation Jesus did not stop Judas even though He knew everything. For this reason, the disciples were able to shout and declare with stronger assurance that Jesus is the Christ.

When Jesus handed the morsel to Judas and gave him permission, Satan went into him. On the surface, Judas sold his teacher, but in reality, he was under the control of Satan. That is why the Scripture says that Satan went into him. In order to kill Jesus, who came as the Savior, the enemy devil and Satan had chosen the evil Judas Iscariot to do his work.

Here, the work of the devil and the work of Satan are different from each other. Satan is like a radio wave that controls the mind and makes one think evil thoughts, and the devil is the one that pushes man to put that evil thought into action. Satan poured into Judas Iscariot the thought of selling his own teacher. The problem here was that because Judas was evil, he accepted this thought, instead of fighting it off. And going beyond the mere thought of selling Jesus, he actually began forming a plan. This is the work of the devil.

This is why Jesus said, *"Did I Myself not choose you, the twelve, and yet one of you is a devil?"* (John 6:70) So an evil person will be controlled by the evil spirit. Therefore we need to pray with zealous fire and be filled with the Holy Spirit and do not let Satan touch our thoughts. After a while, Jesus said to

Judas, "What you do, do quickly."

The Disciples Do Not Understand Jesus' Words

"Now no one of those reclining at the table knew for what purpose He had said this to him. For some were supposing, because Judas had the money box, that Jesus was saying to him, 'Buy the things we have need of for the feast'; or else, that he should give something to the poor. So after receiving the morsel he went out immediately; and it was night" (13:28-30).

The other disciples had no way of knowing what conversation just went on between Jesus and Judas Iscariot. They assumed that Judas Iscariot left early without saying anything to buy some things they needed for the feast, or to help the poor. This was because he was in charge of the money box.

To the disciples' inquiry about who would sell the teacher, Jesus did not answer directly. Instead, He answered with His actions. But no one understood. This is because the fact that Jesus would be sold by the hands of a sinner and die on the cross to fulfill the plan of salvation was a secret that had been hidden since the beginning of time. God made sure that no one knew about it until the plan was finally revealed.

Luke 18:34 says, *"But the disciples understood none of these things, and the meaning of this statement was hidden from them, and they did not comprehend the things that were said."* That is why Jesus was able to bring Judas out into the open and talk about him. No matter how crafty the enemy devil might be, and no matter how hard he tried to get rid of Jesus, God's will stands firm to the end. And the fact that Jesus would appear again through the glory of the resurrection, was a truth that wasn't going to change.

Becoming anxious in fear that his plan has been exposed, Judas Iscariot slowly got up from his seat and slipped outside. The outside had long been dark, and the night air coldly wrapped itself around Judas' heart.

"A New Commandment
I Give to You"

Despite the incredibly heavy demands of the situation, Jesus was rather serene. Since Judas Iscariot left to carry out his scheme, Jesus being captured was just a matter of time. In a little while, Jesus would be turned over to the people who sought to kill Him, and He would have to suffer. But what do you think Jesus did right before all of this?

Jesus Saw the Glory

"Therefore when he had gone out, Jesus said, 'Now is the Son of Man glorified, and God is glorified in Him; if God is glorified in Him, God will also glorify Him in Himself, and will glorify Him immediately'" (13:31-32).

Jesus knew, and so He confessed that by Him being sold into the hands of the wicked and dying on the cross, God's plan would be fulfilled. He knew that after He died on the cross for the sins of mankind and resurrected, the way of salvation will be opened, and then true children of God—who know God's heart—will be gained.

This is what God had been waiting all this time for—each day feeling like a thousand years, and a thousand years feeling like one day. And now, through Jesus, all these plans would be completed. Therefore it is only right that God be glorified. So when Judas Iscariot left to sell out Jesus, it was now as good as done. This is why Jesus said the Son of Man was already glorified.

So what kind of glory did Jesus receive? Even in this world, if someone accomplishes something for the first time, it is considered a glory and honor. Jesus became the first fruits of the resurrection. Jesus gave His life in order to destroy the chasm that formed between God and man, due to man's sin. And by doing so, He brought peace in the relationship between the two entities once again. And because He had no sin, He demolished the power of death and resurrected from the dead and became the first fruits of those asleep (1 Corinthians 15:20).

And He became the glorious Savior who would lead many souls from Hell to Heaven, and from death to eternal life. God made Jesus Christ the only door of salvation (Acts 4:12). Therefore Jesus will receive—now and forever—the glory and thanksgiving from all of God's children who have gained salvation through Him, so how great is that glory?

Jesus Gives a New Commandment

"Little children, I am with you a little while longer.
You will seek Me; and as I said to the Jews, now I also
say to you, 'Where I am going, you cannot come.' A
new commandment I give to you, that you love one
another, even as I have loved you, that you also love
one another. By this all men will know that you are My
disciples, if you have love for one another" (13:33-35).

Jesus had said to the Jews once before, *"Where I am, you
cannot come"* (John 7:34). This is because after dying on
the cross and resurrecting, He would receive a new, spiritual
body and ascend into heaven. Of course, He would be with
the disciples in spirit, confirming the word through signs and
wonders, but He wouldn't be with them in the flesh. After Jesus
resurrects and ascends into heaven, He would not be found or
seen in this world. But there is one way to be one with the Lord.
It is by loving others, as He loves us.

The reason God sent Jesus into this world was because
He loved the people even though they had become sinners.
Through His actions, Jesus also taught the people about God's
love. We must know this love and make sure this love abides in
us (Ephesians 5:1-2).

The more of God's love—the love that waited so long, so
patiently, to gain true children—we have in us, the more souls
we can lead to salvation. Being kind, not acting unbecomingly,
not self-seeking, etc., are fruits of spiritual love. The more of
these fruits we bear, the more completely we can accomplish

God's work. Believers who live like this are the ones God acknowledges as "My true children", and Jesus calls them "My true disciples."

"You Will Deny Me Three Times"

"Simon Peter said to Him, 'Lord, where are You going?' Jesus answered, 'Where I go, you cannot follow Me now; but you will follow later.' Peter said to Him, 'Lord, why can I not follow You right now? I will lay down my life for You.' Jesus answered, 'Will you lay down your life for Me? Truly, truly, I say to you, a rooster will not crow until you deny Me three times'" (13:36-38).

When Jesus talked about dying on the cross, resurrecting, and ascending into heaven, Peter became filled with anxiety, and said. "Lord, where are You going?" "Where I go, you cannot follow Me now; but you will follow later," answered Jesus.

For a period of three years—which is not a short period of time—Peter was always with Jesus. When Jesus went up to the Mount of Transfiguration, and when He brought back to life the daughter of Jairus, the synagogue official, Peter was with Him. He just couldn't understand, of all people, why even he could not be with Jesus. "Lord, why can I not follow You right now? I will lay down my life for You." Peter was just full of confidence. But Jesus shook His head. "A rooster will not crow until you deny Me three times."

Wanting to express his strong will not to leave or deny Jesus, Peter spoke more insistently. "Even if I have to die with You, I will not deny You!" All the other disciples said the same thing (Mark 14:31). But what eventually happened? As soon as Jesus was arrested, three times Peter denied knowing Jesus, and the rest of the disciples all scattered and ran away.

No matter how much we confess with faith, man does not know even his own heart and the confession is nothing unless God acknowledges it.

Chapter 14

Jesus, the Way, the Truth, and the Life

1. Jesus Comforts the Disciples
(14:1-15)

2. Promise of the Helper, the Holy Spirit
(14:16-31)

Jesus Comforts the Disciples

At this time, Jerusalem was slightly filled with suspense. During the public meeting, the Jewish leaders declared that anyone who believed in Jesus would be put out of the synagogue, and the high priests and Pharisees only sought to capture Jesus whenever they had the chance. On the other hand, Jesus kept talking as though He was about to go somewhere. On top of that, Jesus had said one of the disciples would betray Him. The disciples' hearts must have been heavy.

"Believe in God, Believe Also in Me."

"Do not let your heart be troubled; believe in God, believe also in Me. In My Father's house are many dwelling places; if it were not so, I would have told you; for I go to prepare a place for you. If I go and prepare a place for you, I will come again and receive you to Myself, that where I am, there you may be also" (14:1-3).

Jesus gave a message of hope to the disciples who were filled with worries. "Do not let your heart be troubled; believe in God, believe also in Me."

The incredible signs and wonders that Jesus performed were enough evidence that God was with Him. If they truly believed in Jesus, who God was with, what need do they have to worry? Even if they actually saw Jesus' dying on the cross, they didn't have to worry. Jesus wanted His disciples to have the faith to be able to entrust everything to God's will until they saw the glory of the resurrection. So He told them one secret. He told them about the eternal dwelling place in Heaven.

"In My Father's house are many dwelling places." These words capture Jesus' heart, which desires all people to receive salvation. He did not say, "There are many dwelling places in Heaven," but "In My Father's house are many dwelling places." These words also show Jesus' love. God does not want many people to enter into His kingdom just to reign over them as King; He wants many true children with whom He can give and receive love, and live with eternally. That is why Jesus used the words, "My Father's house".

Because Heaven is endlessly large, anyone who abides in God's love can enter into it. Regardless of race, gender, age, or social status, anyone who believes in Jesus as his Savior and lives according to God's Word can enter. When Jesus said, "For I go to prepare a place for you," He meant that in a little while, He would be given as a sacrifice of peace in order to destroy the wall of sin standing between God and man (1 John 2:2). Therefore anyone who believes in Jesus Christ will be forgiven of his sins, receive salvation, and later enter into the beautiful kingdom of God. So this is what Jesus meant as He prepared to take up the cross and said He was going to prepare a place for us.

When the time comes, and the cultivation of man is completed, Jesus will come back for us. The dwelling places in Heaven will also be completed at that time. This is because the dwelling place and rewards each person receives in Heaven depend on how he or she lived in this world. Therefore the cultivation of man must be completed for all these decisions to be finalized in Heaven.

For example, if someone experienced God's grace at one point of his life and served God faithfully and treasured up many rewards in Heaven, but then some time later he went back to the secular world and lost his salvation, everything he might have earned in Heaven goes back to nothing. However, if we keep the faith and strive to the end to live for God's glory, God will remember all these things and give us rewards. Not only that, we will be able to live with God eternally in Heaven. That is why Jesus said, "That where I am, there you may be also." Even if he is saved, his rewards will be reduced to the extent that he has sinned or brought the name of God down.

"I Am the Way, and the Truth, and the Life."

"'And you know the way where I am going.' Thomas said to Him, 'Lord, we do not know where You are going, how do we know the way?' Jesus said to him, 'I am the way, and the truth, and the life; no one comes to the Father but through Me'" (14:4-6).

Jesus knew exactly where He needed to go. "Where I am going" refers to heaven, where God is, and "the way" is the way that Jesus took: from coming into this world as the Son of God, to fulfilling God's will, and finally to His returning back to heaven. The disciples knew better than anyone else, the way that Jesus took. What Jesus said and how He acted, they saw everything so close by, therefore they knew. This is why Jesus said to them, "And you know the way where I am going."

What Jesus said here also means that not only the disciples, but all people who believe in Jesus need to take this way, the way that Jesus took. In order to go this way, we must be pure. We must cast out the evil in our hearts and become pure. The more we accomplish God's holiness, the more we can understand His heart and will, and fulfill that will. Because Jesus had no sin, He was one with God, and He was able to fulfill His will.

In order to go "the way" we must also be the Lord's witnesses to the ends of the earth. Just as Jesus came to this world to save the sinners, we must diligently spread the gospel and lead many people to salvation. When Jesus said the disciples knew where He was going, Thomas looked puzzled.

"Lord, we do not know where You are going, how do we know the way?" Not long ago, when Jesus said let's go to dead Lazarus, Thomas didn't understand Jesus, and he said, "Let's go die with the Lord." Because Thomas had many thoughts of the flesh, he had a hard time understanding Jesus' words. But the other disciples were the same. The atmosphere was heavy, and with so much on their minds, they didn't understand either, but they dared not ask. They were probably glad to hear Thomas asking the question for them. So to these disciples, Jesus spoke in a clear and definite tone: "I am the way, and the truth, and the life; no one comes to the Father but through Me."

What does Jesus mean when He says "the way"? In order to reach a certain destination, we need to go a certain way to get there. Like so, the only way for a child of God to go to Heaven is through Jesus Christ. As it is written, *"And there is salvation in no one else; for there is no other name under heaven that has been given among men by which we must be saved"* (Acts 4:12), Jesus Christ is the way to Heaven, the way to salvation and eternal life.

Then why did Jesus say "I am the truth"? Just as traffic signals and road signs allow us to safely reach our destination, there is something that allows us to safely reach Heaven. And that is "the truth". We need to follow the truth—which is God's Word—in order to reach our destination, Heaven. Jesus was the Word that became flesh and came into this world. And because He fulfilled the Law with love, He called Himself "the truth".

And Jesus also said, "I am the life" because when we believe in Jesus, who died on the cross to take the punishment on behalf of the sinners—whose souls died due to sin—we gain eternal life (1 John 5:12). When we believe in Jesus Christ, we gain new life, and when we live according to His Word, we can reach Heaven, our home.

"Lord, Show Us the Father"

"'If you had known Me, you would have known My Father also; from now on you know Him, and have seen Him.' Philip said to Him, 'Lord, show us the Father, and it is enough for us.' Jesus said to him, 'Have I been so long with you, and yet you have not come to know Me, Philip? He who has seen Me has seen the Father; how can you say, "Show us the Father"?'" (14:7-9).

There is an old saying that if you look at a child, you can know his parents. When you see a son that looks just like his father, it seems as if you're looking at his father. It seems that way even more when you see the son talk, walk, and act the way his father does. As God's Son, how did Jesus show and teach about God?

First, by preaching the gospel of Heaven, He showed who God is, and how we ought to live. He taught about God's true will according to the Law; but He didn't stop there. Through His actions, He made us feel God's love.

And without any hesitation, Jesus reached out to those who were neglected by society. He pulled out those souls that were drowning in the deep pool of sin and sickness. Even the lepers whose skin was decaying and oozing with pus, Jesus did not consider them unclean. He either commanded with His words, or even put His hands on them to heal them. So whenever Jesus healed the sick and the infirm, He did it with much love; therefore the people felt the warm love of Jesus permeating into their hearts.

This is why when Jesus spoke about God, the people were able to have faith in the fact that God is a God of love, compassion, and mercy. Through their encounter with Jesus, they felt as though they met and saw God. Jesus said, "From now on you know Him, and have seen Him." Even now, we are able to know about God through the life and teachings of Jesus.

The reason Jesus used the words "From now on", was because at that time, one could not say that the disciples truly knew God. Because they hadn't yet witnessed Jesus' execution on the cross and His resurrection, they did not have complete faith yet. As if to prove this, Philip said with haste, "Lord, show us the Father."

Phillip, like Peter, was from the town of Bethsaida, and he was a very logical and practical man. Even when Jesus fed thousands of people with just two fish and five loaves of bread, he was able to quickly calculate how much food they needed, and how much money was needed to buy it. So when he was told that seeing Jesus was seeing God, he could not understand. People like this, who try to understand everything based on their own standards and thoughts, have a hard time understanding spiritual significances, and so they likewise have a hard time gaining faith.

Even today, there are so many cases where people say they believe in God, but they don't really know who God is, let alone understand His heart and will. They see God solely through their own spiritual frameworks, and they think, "The God I believe in is like this." This is just like a frog in a well thinking the sky right above him is the entire world.

That is why they fail to give and receive a greater amount of love from God, and when they see someone that is receiving a great amount of love from God, they consider them strange. So when Jesus asked, "Have I been so long with you, and yet you have not come to know Me, Philip? He who has seen Me has seen the Father; how can you say, 'Show us the Father'?" He was speaking to all people with belief like Philip.

"The Father Abiding in Me Does His works"

"Do you not believe that I am in the Father, and the Father is in Me? The words that I say to you I do not speak on My own initiative, but the Father abiding in Me does His works. Believe Me that I am in the Father and the Father is in Me; otherwise believe because of the works themselves" (14:10-11).

Jesus mentioned earlier that whoever saw Him saw the Father. Why do you suppose He said that? This is because Jesus is in God, and God is in Jesus; therefore They are completely one. Even through powerful works He showed that He was one with God. He healed all kinds of diseases and made infirmities whole again. Even the words that He spoke were not by His own initiative, but spoken by the Father who was abiding in Him (John 12:49-50).

And because He was one with God, Jesus was able to take the excruciating way of fulfilling the plan of salvation by death on the cross. Jesus was already one with God at heart and will in the desire to save the souls dying in sin. That is why He was able to fearlessly take the way which, to human eyes, looked extremely difficult. Just as we can decipher a tree by its fruit, when we look at the things Jesus did, we can see and believe that He is in God, and God is in Him.

He Who Believes in Me Will Do Greater Works

"Truly, truly, I say to you, he who believes in Me, the works that I do, he will do also; and greater works than these he will do; because I go to the Father" (14:12).

In Hebrews 11:1, faith is defined as *"the assurance of things hoped for, the conviction of things not seen."* In Mark 9:23 it says, *"All things are possible to him who believes."* Therefore when we have true faith in Jesus, we can do the works that Jesus did, and even greater works as well.

But why did Jesus have to go to the Father for these things to happen?

When we dig up peanuts or potatoes, if we uproot just one vine, many of the produce on the vine can be reaped at the same time. At first, only one peanut or one piece of a potato is planted, but later it yields much more. Likewise, Jesus was like a single seed sown into this world for God's kingdom. Just as a seed produces much more fruit only after it loses its own form, only after Jesus sacrificed Himself completely could so many children of God be gained.

The moment that Jesus finished His ministry here on earth and ascended into heaven was the moment a new fire was ignited to complete the kingdom of God. This is why Jesus left behind His twelve disciples. And even after that, much of God's work was done through the disciples of those twelve disciples. In reality, we can see that those believers who were one with Jesus in faith, accomplished many powerful works of God just like Jesus.

If you look at the book of Acts, it says that when Peter preached, there were added about three thousand souls. He also healed a person crippled from birth, and raised a person from the dead, and he performed many other miraculous signs. Because these signs were performed through Peter, many people received salvation, and God was greatly glorified. The apostle Paul also performed signs and wonders, and he not only carried out, but also left an astounding impact on the ministry of spreading the gospel. It all happened just as Jesus said, "And greater works than these he will do."

"If You Ask Me Anything in My Name, I Will Do It"

"Whatever you ask in My name, that will I do, so that the Father may be glorified in the Son. If you ask Me anything in My name, I will do it. If you love Me, you will keep My commandments" (14:13-15).

When we pray, we must pray in the name of 'Jesus Christ the Savior', and we must believe that we will receive an answer. Because God is all-powerful, whatever we ask for in the name of Jesus Christ, He can give us. That is why Jesus said, "Whatever you ask in My name, that will I do." And to better understand why He said, "so that the Father may be glorified in the Son," let's take a look at an illustration.

Let's say that a respectable man who is the owner of a very big company wants to pass everything down to his son. Now if the son's ideals and wisdom are like that of his father, and he runs the company well, and develops it to make it even greater, then his father will be very pleased. And other people will praise the son and say, "He is just like his father." Likewise, when many works of God happen through the name of Jesus Christ, God's kingdom and sphere of influence are enlarged, and God is ultimately glorified.

And the reason Jesus said once again, "If you ask Me anything in My name, I will do it," was to emphasize one more time, the fact that God can do anything.

Now of course this does not mean that just because you pray and ask for something in the name of Jesus Christ you'll receive everything you ask for. Just as it is written, *"Beloved, if our heart does not condemn us, we have confidence before God; and whatever we ask we receive from Him, because we keep His commandments and do the things that are pleasing in His sight"* (1 John 3:21-22), we must live according to God's Word, above all. As we want to listen to the person whom we love, and want to do anything they ask for, if we love the Lord, we would obey the commands of God which the Lord taught us. This is the evidence of our love for God.

Promise of the Helper,
the Holy Spirit

Jesus knew that after He completes the mission of fulfilling the plan of salvation for mankind, He would return to the Father. This was already planned from the beginning. However, one thing made His heart heavy. Every time He looked at His disciples, He felt as though He was leaving a flock of sheep in the midst of wolves, and He felt great sadness. In order to comfort the disciples, He gave them the hope of Heaven, faith and prayer, and how to have victory through love. And then Jesus promised them another Helper.

Another Helper

"I will ask the Father, and He will give you another

Helper, that He may be with you forever; that is the Spirit of truth, whom the world cannot receive, because it does not see Him or know Him, but you know Him because He abides with you and will be in you" (14:16-17).

The 'Helper' here means "A person who speaks on another person's behalf, and persuades or advises them to realize what is right and wrong," or "one who makes recommendations, gives support, strength, and comfort." In this respect, Jesus also led a life of a Helper. He was a prophet of God, He was a mediator who helped people realize their sins, and with God's heart He healed the wounded and suffering souls while comforting them with the gospel of Heaven.

That is why Jesus did not simply call the Holy Spirit, who would be protecting and teaching the disciples "A Helper", but "Another Helper". As "God's heart", the Holy Spirit is also called "the Spirit of Truth". The Holy Spirit knocks on each person's heart so he or she can enter through the door of salvation that was opened by Jesus Christ. For those who are good at heart and who receive Jesus Christ, the Holy Spirit dwells in them. He helps them understand the providence of the cross of Jesus Christ, and He helps people feel God's heart.

The Bible says the presence of the Holy Spirit was "descending as a dove" (Matthew 3:16), and *"...there appeared to them tongues as of fire distributing themselves, and they rested on each one of them"* (Acts 2:3). The Holy Spirit works differently with each person's personality and circumstances so he or she can best understand God's love. However, because people of this world love the darkness more than the light, they cannot receive the Holy Spirit, which is a part of God, who is Light. Just as one cannot see the wind, even though He exists, these kinds of people cannot feel the Holy Spirit.

The Holy Spirit Who Indwells

"I will not leave you as orphans; I will come to you. After a little while the world will no longer see Me, but you will see Me; because I live, you will live also. In that day you will know that I am in My Father, and you in Me, and I in you" (14:18-20).

Without Jesus, the disciples would be like orphans that had lost their parents. But Jesus, who is compassionate and loving, would never leave them that way. Yes, they would be separated once He died on the cross, but He let them know that the separation is only for a little while, and He promised to return.

"I will not leave you as orphans; I will come to you." And just as He said, after His resurrection, Jesus returned to visit His disciples on several occasions, and He even appeared to five hundred brethren at the same time (1 Corinthians 15:6). But when He said, "I will come to you," He didn't just mean appearing before them after the resurrection. There is another deep meaning behind this statement, which is that once Jesus fulfills the plan of salvation, He and His disciples can be together for eternity.

Right before His crucifixion, Jesus said, "Because I live," because He had complete assurance that the providence of God would be fulfilled.

The enemy devil and Satan thought that by killing Jesus, the Messiah, everything would be over. However, because he killed Jesus, who had no sin, he ultimately broke the law of God that says "For the wages of sin is death". Satan had dug his own grave. As a result, anyone who is spiritually one with the Lord, who became the firstfruits of the resurrection, is free from the law of sin and death, and receives eternal life. Because the Lord resurrected, the doorway to life has been opened to all of us as well.

Jesus said, "In that day you will know that I am in My Father, and you in Me, and I in you." Here, "In that day" refers to the day Jesus resurrected after destroying the power of death. Even though Jesus is originally one with God, only after fully completing the mission He received from God, did He say "I am in the Father". At this time, Jesus was in the same state as a son who accomplished what his father wanted, and was therefore able to look into his father's face with joy and confidence.

'You are in Me' signifies our faith in the Lord. When we believe in Jesus Christ, we can live in the Lord. This is not faith based on what we know in our heads, but spiritual faith, which does not change—no matter what the circumstances. Only when we have this kind of faith can we say we are *in the Lord*.

And the reason why Jesus said, 'I am in you,' is because God sends the Holy Spirit to dwell in the hearts of those people who believe in Jesus as their Savior. We cannot see the Holy Spirit with our eyes, but He actually abides in us. He helps us realize God's heart and will, and He also helps us feel the love of Jesus Christ.

He Who Keeps the Commandments with the Holy Spirit's Help

"He who has My commandments and keeps them is the one who loves Me; and he who loves Me will be loved by My Father, and I will love him and will disclose Myself to him" (14:21).

This verse tells us what it means to 'love Jesus with the help of the Holy Spirit'. If we say we love Jesus, but do not keep His commandments, then that means we don't truly love Him. Loving someone simply with our words alone is like an empty echo. It has no real value. That is why after explaining about being one with the Father, the Son, and the Holy Spirit, Jesus emphasized, "He who has My commandments and keeps them is the one who loves Me."

If, by faith, someone has a trusting relationship with the Lord, and truly loves the Lord, he will take His words to heart and try to live them out. He won't simply obey the words just to be obedient—he will understand why Jesus said those words and so he will carry them out with joy and thanksgiving.

Just as we beautify ourselves to go meet someone who we love in the physical world, if we truly love the Lord, we will want to get rid of our old self, which was one with the world, and naturally begin resembling the Lord. The way we speak, the way we walk, and each act that we do, will become holy and wholesome, to resemble Christ. Only those who continue to change like this—with the help of the Holy Spirit—can truly say they love the Lord.

If we look at the Bible, God expresses exceptional love to those people who keep His commands because of their love for Him. To Abraham, who was willing to sacrifice his only son, Isaac, God gave him the great blessing of becoming the father of faith, the root of blessings. Daniel, who loved God more than his own life, received exceptional protection, even from the mouths of hungry lions. He was able to show God's glory in a great way all over the country.

God doesn't just one-sidedly receive the love that His children give to Him with all of their heart, will, and life. Without doubt, He shows us the evidence of His love as well. Therefore, we can abide by His Word with even greater joy and thanksgiving.

I Will Be With You in the Name of the Father, the Son, and the Holy Spirit

"Judas (not Iscariot) said to Him, 'Lord, what then has happened that You are going to disclose Yourself to us and not to the world?' Jesus answered and said to him, 'If anyone loves Me, he will keep My word; and My Father will love him, and We will come to him and

make Our abode with him. He who does not love Me does not keep My words; and the word which you hear is not Mine, but the Father's who sent Me" (14:22-24).

Judas, not Iscariot, was one of Jesus' twelve disciples. He was the son of James, and was also called "Thaddeus" (Luke 6:16). Unable to understand the spiritual meaning behind Jesus' words, Judas asked why He disclosed Himself to the disciples but not to the world. But in reality, it was not that Jesus did not disclose Himself to the world—it was that the people of the world did not recognize Him. Jesus opened the eyes of a blind man, and thus revealed Himself; however, the Jews accused Him as they would a sinner. They did not understand Jesus' words, which contained true life in them. Instead, they mocked and persecuted Him.

On the contrary, people with good hearts understood His words, and they took the life in His words as their own and applied it to their lives. Only people like these confess Jesus Christ as their Lord and can call God their Father. That is why Jesus said once again, that to love Him is to keep His words, and that to him who keeps His words, "We will come to him and make Our abode with him."

Here, the first person plural refers to 'God the Father, who is the Word', 'Jesus Christ the Savior', and the 'Holy Spirit'. When the Word is in us, and we keep the Father's commands, the Father is in us, and we are one with Him, which makes us His true children. 'We', meaning God, Jesus Christ, and the Holy Spirit as one, when They abide in our hearts, not just one part of the Father, or the Son, or the Holy Spirit, but the complete heart of God the Trinity, is inscribed into our hearts.

People who revere God and follow the truth come before Jesus and they love to listen to the Word. They are enlightened in their hearts and they know Jesus is the Christ. This is because they receive Jesus' words as the very words from God.

The Ministry of the Holy Spirit, the Helper

"These things I have spoken to you while abiding with you. But the Helper, the Holy Spirit, whom the Father will send in My name, He will teach you all things, and bring to your remembrance all that I said to you" (14:25-26).

So why did God have to wait until after Jesus completed His mission in this world before sending the Holy Spirit in the name of Jesus Christ? The Holy Spirit is 'God's Spirit which is holy'; therefore He cannot dwell in sinners. Only those who have been forgiven of their sins through the blood of Jesus can receive the Holy Spirit. Because Jesus became the propitiation and made peace between man and God, the Holy Spirit— whom God sent—could now dwell in our hearts.

This does not mean that there was no work of the Holy Spirit in the Old Testament times before Jesus came. In those days, in the name of the Spirit of God or the Spirit of the LORD, God moved the hearts of prophets, or His people to do His work. Because this was before men were forgiven of their sins through the blood of Jesus Christ, the Holy Spirit could not dwell inside of people's hearts; instead, He moved people from the outside so they could carry out His work.

'God will send the Holy Spirit in Jesus Christ's name', means that the Holy Spirit, being 'of the same Spirit' as Jesus, will come in Jesus' place. The Holy Spirit carries out a truly important ministry. One of the most important tasks He has is that "He will teach you all things, and bring to your remembrance all that I said to you."

The Holy Spirit moves each believer and helps him to have spiritual enlightenment so he can know and understand all of Jesus' parables, and God's heart. Even if someone claims to have received many of Jesus' teachings, if he does not receive the workings of the Holy Spirit, then all of those remain as mere knowledge. However, when someone is full of the Holy Spirit, and is moved by Him, he can understand not only God's words spoken through parables; but also the secrets of the spiritual world.

The Peace Given By the Holy Spirit, Our Helper

"Peace I leave with you; My peace I give to you; not as the world gives do I give to you. Do not let your heart be troubled, nor let it be fearful. You heard that I said to you, 'I go away, and I will come to you.' If you loved Me, you would have rejoiced because I go to the Father, for the Father is greater than I" (14:27-28).

People want to live a peaceful life, but as long as we're in this world, anxieties and worries will never end. There are so many times when one minute we are in a great mood, and then the next minute we're fighting and quarreling. No matter where we look, it's very hard to find true peace. However, the peace that God gives us is true, and it is eternal.

When Jesus told His disciples that after He was going to be betrayed and sold out and that He was going to go to a place where they would not be able to follow, His disciples could not rid themselves of their worries and fears. Even though Jesus promised to send the Holy Spirit to them, because they did not understand the spiritual meaning of this, they couldn't help but worry. Even still, Jesus did not scold them for not understanding Him. Instead He promised them true peace that the world cannot give them.

Jesus told them to rejoice because the Holy Spirit, the Helper, would come after He is gone to the Father. He means the Holy Spirit will come into their hearts and indwell in them. So, though Jesus would not be able to abide with them in the body anymore, the Holy Spirit will dwell in them all the time. In this sense, the disciples should have rejoiced when Jesus said, "I go to the Father, for the Father is greater than I" because God the Almighty will send the Holy Spirit as the Helper and lead them to the end.

The Crucifixion and the Disciples' Faith

"Now I have told you before it happens, so that when

it happens, you may believe. I will not speak much more with you, for the ruler of the world is coming, and he has nothing in Me; but so that the world may know that I love the Father, I do exactly as the Father commanded Me. Get up, let us go from here" (14:29-31).

There are two reasons why, after completing the Passover meal, Jesus told His disciples about His death on the cross before it actually happened. First, it was so that after the mission on the cross was completed, the disciples could believe, and second, so they knew that Jesus' death was a part of God's plan.

The reason Jesus was captured and crucified by the 'ruler of the world', or those with power, like the high priest, the Pharisees, and the scribes, was not because He did not have power Himself. Because He was one at heart with God in not wanting to see even one soul perishing, He completely obeyed God's will and took all the suffering. Jesus died on the cross even though He had no sin in order to demonstrate God's love (Romans 5:8).

This is why Jesus said, "... and [the ruler of the world] has nothing in Me; but so that the world may know that I love the Father, I do exactly as the Father commanded Me." Jesus loved the Father, so He simply carried out His command. He was not shaken by the powers of this world. That's why He said "He has nothing in Me." Only after Jesus resurrected and ascended into heaven did the disciples realize this providence of God and gain the true faith which allowed them to dedicate their entire lives to being powerful witnesses of the Lord.

Chapter 15

Jesus Is the True Vine

The Parable of the Vine
and the Branches

Having the Passover meal with His disciples, Jesus told them
something that was like His last will. A person's last words
leave a lasting impression on those who hear them. Even people
who aren't usually good at listening to other people will pay
attention and embed the last words of someone they know in
their hearts.

To explain His relationship with His disciples, Jesus said that
He is the vine, God is the vinedresser, and that His disciples are
the branches on the vine. The time continued to pass as Jesus'
heart ached for His disciples as He had to leave them, and the
disciples' hearts ached for their teacher as they learned of His
imminent death.

The Vinedresser and the Vine

> "I am the true vine, and My Father is the vinedresser. Every branch in Me that does not bear fruit, He takes away; and every branch that bears fruit, He prunes it so that it may bear more fruit" (15:1-2).

Jesus used the parable of the vine and the branches so His disciples could better understand Him. Grape vines are very common in Israel. In the summer, Israel gets little rain, and its temperatures are high and dry, so its conditions are perfect for producing grapes. But even if you plant the best variety of plants in the best possible soil, it is still the farmer's role that is most important in producing good fruit. Depending on what the farmer does, the yield and grade of the crops vary.

Jesus used the illustration of God being the farmer, and Himself being the grape vine that was planted in this world according to God's will, in order to show that all the authority belongs to God. From the beginning of time, God had the plan of sending Jesus into this world to prepare the way of salvation. And when the time was right, God carried out His plan. Then why did Jesus compare Himself to a grape vine, of all plants?

This is because the grape juice that comes from the grape symbolizes Jesus' blood. As He shared the wine with His disciples during the last supper, Jesus said, *"This cup which is poured out for you is the new covenant in My blood"* (Luke 22:20). And the reason He called Himself the true grape vine is because as the truth itself, Jesus is fundamentally God, who is eternally unchanging.

Jesus also used this parable because of a grape vine's characteristic of producing many fruits. A grape is a fruit composed of a cluster of fruits. In the same way, we, as the children of God who are all connected through Jesus Christ and faith, also bear fruits. As our soul prospers, we can lead many souls to salvation and we can bear such fruits as the nine fruits of the Holy Spirit, the fruits of love (found in the Chapter of Love), the Beatitudes, and fruits of the Light.

Using this illustration of the grape vine, Jesus totally acknowledged and lifted up God, the Governor of all things. Since God provides the nutrients and perfect amounts of water, sun, and air necessary for the fruits to blossom, complete sovereignty belongs to Him.

The farmer makes sure the tree is in good shape, and he prunes the branches so the tree can bear good fruit. In the same way, a person who professes to believe in Jesus Christ but does not live according to the Word of truth ends up falling away from Jesus Christ. When we first look at the verse, "Every branch in Me that does not bear fruit, He takes away," it may seem that, comparing a farmer to God metaphorically, God just indiscriminately cuts down any branch He wants. However, this is not the case.

God, who wants all people to be saved, will never be the one who would cut off anyone first. Here the 'branches that are cut' actually refer to those people who fail to live according to God's Word and fall away from the way of truth on their own accord. On the other hand, those people who reflect upon themselves using His Word and who try to renew and improve themselves,

God holds up with His power. Furthermore, He gives them the opportunity to discover any kinds of evil they may have in their hearts, so they can cast them off.

For example, when a parent discovers that his child has a strong potential in some area or skill he thinks, "If this child receives special support in this area, he will be very successful." He will then ensure that his child receives special education and training in that area. Likewise, when God sees one of His children trying very hard to cast away their sins to become sanctified, He leads them to a higher, more wholesome dimension by allowing them to experience some tribulations.

As written in James 1:2-4, *"Consider it all joy, my brethren, when you encounter various trials, knowing that the testing of your faith produces endurance. And let endurance have its perfect result, so that you may be perfect and complete, lacking in nothing,"* through trials, people are trained and refined to become more perfect children of God. This is like the process of pruning.

The Grape Vine and Its Branches

"You are already clean because of the word which I have spoken to you. Abide in Me, and I in you. As the branch cannot bear fruit of itself unless it abides in the vine, so neither can you unless you abide in Me. I am the vine, you are the branches; he who abides in Me and I in him, he bears much fruit, for apart from Me you can do nothing. If anyone does not abide in Me, he is thrown away as a branch and dries up; and they gather them, and cast them into the fire and they are burned" (15:3-6).

Because the disciples had not received the Holy Spirit yet, they could not understand the spiritual meaning behind the parable of the grape vine. As if their minds were covered by a thick fog, they just couldn't grasp it. But knowing that the disciples would understand everything later on, once they received the Holy Spirit, Jesus continued to teach them.

"You are already clean because of the word which I have spoken to you..." This passage means that Jesus has the power to forgive sins (Matthew 9:6). As written in 1 John 1:7, *"But if we walk in the Light as He Himself is in the Light, we have fellowship with one another, and the blood of Jesus His Son cleanses us from all sin,"* when we accept the Lord and live in the midst of the Light, we are forgiven of our sins, we receive salvation, and we can go to Heaven.

But there is a precondition to this. Only when we live in the midst of the Light, or according to God's Word, can we have fellowship with God, and only by the blood of Jesus Christ, can we be cleansed. Let's say there is a person who has a tendency to hit others when he is angry. He hits because he cannot control his anger. Let's say he hit someone, later feels remorse for what he's done, and he apologizes. But if after he apologizes, he again uses violence whenever he becomes angry, could he receive true forgiveness?

In the same manner, just because you confess your sins before God, you should not stop there. The actions you take afterwards are more important. This is because true repentance does not end with just confessing your sins with your lips, but in completely turning away from your sin.

Moreover, another reason Jesus told His disciples that they were 'already clean' was because they can receive the blessing of sanctification by God's grace—not only because they will be forgiven of their sins, but also because they could cast off the sins inside of their hearts and become clean. Jesus said, "You are already clean because of the word which I have spoken to you," but at that time, the disciples had not received the Holy Spirit. But He also knew that later when the disciples did receive the Holy Spirit, they would then understand everything He taught them, and would be transformed into clean vessels.

No matter how strong a branch may be, it cannot bear fruit if it separates from the vine. Just so, we can only receive life and bear much fruit when we abide in Jesus, who is the true vine.

To 'abide in Jesus' means to 'live according to God's Word,' which is the truth. So the opposite is such that if we do not live in the truth, we can only drift away from Jesus. It is just as written in 1 John 2:15, *"Do not love the world nor the things in the world. If anyone loves the world, the love of the Father is not in him."*

Just as a pot of boiling water eventually becomes cool if it isn't constantly heated, if our heart is focused on the world, our love for God begins to cool, and we eventually drift away from the truth. The problem here is that the cooling process happens slowly and subtly, so we may not even realize what is happening.

Then ultimately, the Holy Spirit is quenched from our hearts, and we may even end up losing our salvation.

A farmer plants a tree in order to reap its fruit. Branches that do not bear fruit, or branches that fall off the vine are useless. Branches of a grape vine are especially bent and crooked, so if it doesn't bear fruit, the only use for it is for firewood. This is the same for our spiritual lives as well. A person who grows closer and closer to the world and falls away from Jesus eventually goes to the way of death, and ultimately falls into the fire of Hell.

The Secret to Bearing Much Fruit

"If you abide in Me, and My words abide in you, ask whatever you wish, and it will be done for you. My Father is glorified by this, that you bear much fruit, and so prove to be My disciples" (15:7-8).

Those people who follow after Jesus' heart and are totally one with Him do not seek their own selfish desires. Instead, they earnestly lift up prayers of love for God's kingdom, and for lost souls. God is pleased with this kind of people, and so whatever they ask, He gives them (1 John 5:14). Therefore, those people who live according to God's Word and pray for the fulfillment of God's kingdom and His righteousness, bear much fruit. To 'bear much fruit' means to show not only the nine fruits of the Holy Spirit, the Chapter of Love in 1 Corinthians, and the Beatitudes; but also means to show God's power and authority through signs and wonders.

Just as many people gave glory to God when Jesus showed God's power through signs and wonders, we, as children of God, should bear much fruit and give glory to God, too. That is when God will say, "I am so pleased to gain such true children," and feel rewarded and joyful for cultivating man. This is what Jesus meant when He said, "My Father is glorified by this." Also, the act of circumcising our hearts through God's Word and becoming more like Him by itself, gives glory to God, and brings joy to His heart.

And anyone who believes in Jesus Christ and abides in His words and gives glory to God together with Him, regardless of what the period of time the person lives in, that person can be called the "Lord's disciple". Being the "Lord's disciple" means having the promise of living with God in the midst of His glory, upon entering Heaven.

Abide In My Love

"Just as the Father has loved Me, I have also loved you; abide in My love. If you keep My commandments, you will abide in My love; just as I have kept My Father's commandments and abide in His love. These things I have spoken to you so that My joy may be in you, and that your joy may be made full" (15:9-11).

How would parents feel if they had to send their loving son to a place with danger lurking in every corner? They would probably rather go there themselves, and not send their son. If possible, parents would rather experience pain themselves if that meant sparing their child from it. So how do you think God felt when He sent His Son Jesus into this world full of sin?

Because God loved us, even while we were going to the way of death, He sent His only begotten Son to us. Because Jesus knew God's will better than anyone else, He loved us and the plan of salvation through the cross could be fulfilled. To those of us who are clothed with this great love of God, Jesus said, "I have also loved you; abide in My love."

In Matthew chapter 22, one of the experts in the law wanted to test Jesus with this question: *"Teacher, which is the greatest commandment in the Law?"* (v. 36) At this, Jesus gave him this clear answer: *"Love the Lord your God with all your heart and with all your soul and with all your mind. This is the first and greatest commandment. And the second is like it: 'Love your neighbor as yourself'"* (v. 37-39).

Jesus showed this to us through His actions. Casting aside His glory in Heaven to come into this world, and taking all the pain and suffering upon the cross was all possible because of His love for God and His love for us.

The evidence of our love for God is shown by our obedience to His commandments (1 John 5:3). Commandments of God refer to all the words recorded in the 66 books of the Bible and those who try to live according to the Word of God come to increasingly understand the heart of God. In the process of understanding and acting upon His Word, they can realize the love of God and measure the depths of His heart. This is why Jesus made this promise, "If you keep My commandments, you will abide in My love; just as I have kept My Father's commandments and abide in His love."

As He spent His last night in this world, Jesus wanted to show God's love to His disciples more than anything else. And He taught them that His suffering on the cross was the way of completing God's plan of salvation, and that through this process, mankind, whose ultimate destiny was death due to sin, could earn the privilege of becoming God's children and eventually go to Heaven. Jesus wanted the disciples not to become alarmed and dismayed by the events that were about to take place, but rather to receive them with joy.

"You Are My Friends If You Do What I Command You"

"This is My commandment, that you love one another, just as I have loved you. Greater love has no one than this, that one lay down his life for his friends. You are My friends if you do what I command you" (15:12-14).

To obey Jesus' commandment is to love others as Jesus loved us. This love is a spiritual love, or sacrificial love where one can lay down his life for God, His kingdom, His righteousness, and even a fellow brother. The more sin and evil we cast out and become sanctified, the more spiritual love we can have in our hearts. Only when we have cast out hate, jealousy, envy, and the like, can we truly love our neighbors as ourselves and serve them with love.

So when Jesus told us to "love one another", the deeper message contained in this three-word phrase is Jesus' sincere will and desire for the children of God to cultivate their hearts with the truth and become more like Him. Friends know and understand one another, and friends love one another. A true friend will consider his friend's business as his own and will be willing to sacrifice for that friend. And if that friend was even willing to sacrifice his own life for his friend, there would be no greater love than that.

So why do you think Jesus said what He said?

Jesus wanted to become a spiritual friend not only to His disciples, but also to all the people who would later come to read His words. But there is one condition: Jesus said, "You are My friends if you do what I command you." This means that if we want to become spiritual friends with Jesus, we need to know and understand God's every word, which is the truth, and live according to the truth. Just as Jesus sacrificed His own life and showed us the greatest love, only when we fill ourselves up with this great love, can we become spiritual friends with Jesus.

The Difference between Slave and Friend

"No longer do I call you slaves, for the slave does not know what his master is doing; but I have called you friends, for all things that I have heard from My Father I have made known to you" (15:15).

In Romans 5:12, it is written, *"Therefore, just as through one man sin entered into the world, and death through sin, and so death spread to all men, because all sinned—"* After Adam sinned, all of his descendents after him were born with a sinful nature; and as sinners, they became slaves to the enemy devil and Satan.

But anyone who becomes free from sin by salvation through the cross of Jesus Christ is no longer a slave to sin; but a child of God, born again of the Holy Spirit. Romans 8:15 says, *"For you have not received a spirit of slavery leading to fear again, but you have received a spirit of adoption as sons by which we cry out, 'Abba! Father!'"*

As a "slave" does not know the master's heart, a person who is a slave to sin does not know Jesus' words or God's love. He does not know the heart of God, who cultivates man, or about Jesus, who came into this world, knowing the Father's heart. With these words, Jesus encouraged His disciples that once He dies on the cross, and the sin of mankind is forgiven, they should never again become slaves to sin. This was a message not only to the disciples, but to everyone who accepted the Lord, up to this day.

According to these words, God shows His providence of salvation in the cross to anyone who is born again by the Holy Spirit and who becomes a friend of Jesus. Just as we can tell our secrets to our trusted friends, God will let them know not only about the deepest secrets of the spiritual world, but also about the events to come. Especially in this day and age, which is the era of the Holy Spirit, one can even come to understand the deepest part of the heart of God.

The Reason Jesus Chose and Taught His Disciples

"You did not choose Me but I chose you, and appointed you that you would go and bear fruit, and that your fruit would remain, so that whatever you ask of the Father in My name He may give to you. This I command you, that you love one another" (15:16-17).

How did the twelve disciples come to serve Jesus? Jesus called them first. He said, "Follow Me," to Peter and Andrew, who were fishing in the sea, and He told them that they would become fishers of men. He also called James and John, who were mending their nets with their father (Matthew 4:18-22). He also told Philip and Levi the tax collector, "Follow Me!" (Mark 2:14; John 1:43)

So the grace of salvation was not given to us because we first sought God and asked Him for it. As it is written in Ephesians 2:8, *"For by grace you have been saved through faith; and that not of yourselves, it is the gift of God,"* it was given to us without any cost, by God, who wanted to gain true children.

This was so that we could bear fruit. We "bear fruit" when we transform ourselves through God's Word. For example, a person who could not love transforms into a loving person, a person who could not understand others transforms into an understanding person. He will not only try to understand others when they act rudely, but also try to help them. A person who bears fruits of truth like this can receive anything when he asks in the name of Jesus Christ.

When Jesus said, "This I command you," He was telling us to 'bear the fruit of truth through God's Word and become sanctified.' And the reason He told us to transform ourselves with God's Word, which is the truth, was so that we can "love one another".

A person who loves with spiritual love will be sanctified by being armed with the truth; and he will be at peace with everyone and be acknowledged before God. The more we recover God's image which we had once lost, the more spiritual love can come out of us so we can even love our enemies. This is because the core of God's heart is love. Therefore the ultimate reason Jesus said to "love one another" was so that we, as children of God, can recover what was once lost—God's image in us.

Jesus wanted to teach this core love of God to the disciples and all of God's children. Anyone who has received God's grace, which He gave without any cost, should transform his heart with the truth. The more truth we have in our hearts, the more power we have to love one another.

The World and the Disciples

In Matthew chapter 4, there is an account where Jesus was tempted by Satan for 40 days before He started His public ministry. At this time, Satan tempted Him, showing Him all the kingdoms of the world and their glory: *"All these things I will give You, if You fall down and worship me"* (v. 9). Of course Jesus cast Satan away with the Word of God, but this event shows us that the enemy Satan has the power and authority over all the kingdoms of this world.

God gave Adam the authority to subdue and rule over the world, but because of his disobedience, he became a slave to sin. Therefore Adam's authority had to be passed on to the enemy devil and Satan. If a freeman becomes a slave to someone, all his rights are now given over to his master (Romans 6:16). And this is also the reason the enemy devil and Satan are referred to as the "rulers of the darkness of this age" just as recorded in Ephesians 6:12 NKJV, which reads, *"For we do not wrestle against flesh and blood, but against principalities, against powers, against the rulers of the darkness of this age, against spiritual hosts of wickedness in the heavenly places."*

Why the World Hates You

"If the world hates you, you know that it has hated Me before it hated you. If you were of the world, the world would love its own; but because you are not of the world, but I chose you out of the world, because of this the world hates you" (15:18-19).

Just as the light and the dark cannot be one, God and this world that came under the authority of the enemy devil and Satan, cannot be one. This is another reason why the more we obey God's Word and live in the truth, the more distant we become from this secular world.

On the contrary, a person who loves the world becomes further and further away from God; and the more he chases after his fleshly desires, the more he falls into the slough of sin. The deeper one falls, the happier the enemy devil and Satan becomes. This is why Jesus said, "If you were of the world, the world would love its own."

Naturally, the world hates the ones chosen by God, the ones who accept Jesus as their Savior and chase after the truth. There are times in our spiritual walk, when we experience difficulties or hardships just for the sole reason we're living according to God's Word. We might be trying to make others more comfortable by serving them, but they may do whatever they can to find fault in everything we do. This is the result of the enemy devil and Satan controlling the evil people belonging to them.

Therefore it is written in 1 John 3:13, *"Do not be surprised, brethren, if the world hates you."* Even though we are afflicted at times while striving to live in the truth, God will ultimately work for the good of those who trust in His name. So, all circumstances actually end up as a blessing.

> **"Remember the word that I said to you, 'A slave is not greater than his master.' If they persecuted Me, they will also persecute you; if they kept My word, they will keep yours also" (15:20).**

'Slave' refers to the evil spirits that have control over the kingdom of the air, and the enemy devil and Satan that are the rulers over the world of darkness. 'Master' refers to God the Father. "A slave is not greater than his master" means that the powers of the evil spirits that control the air are not greater than the power of God. Therefore, we, the children of God, need not be scared, or fear anything in this world.

However, just as it is written, "If they persecuted Me, they will also persecute you," the enemy devil and Satan will do whatever they can until the end of the world to tempt one more person into the kingdom of darkness. At times Satan will control those people who do not know God, or people of little faith to persecute and bring hardship to the children of God. But because God, who has greater power than the enemy devil and Satan, leads and protects us, we can be bold and courageous.

Then what do you think Jesus meant when He said, "If they kept My word, they will keep yours also"? This means that even though we may face persecutions and intimidations, we should have faith in our God, who has greater power than all the things of this world, and we should continue to spread His word and show His love with boldness and without fear. Then we will be protected and guarded by God's power, and we will be able to give glory to God.

> "But all these things they will do to you for My name's sake, because they do not know the One who sent Me. If I had not come and spoken to them, they would not have sin, but now they have no excuse for their sin. He who hates Me hates My Father also. If I had not done among them the works which no one else did, they would not have sin; but now they have both seen and hated Me and My Father as well. But they have done this to fulfill the word that is written in their Law, 'THEY HATED ME WITHOUT A CAUSE'" (15:21-25).

The Pharisees and the high priests claimed to fervently study and keep the words of the Bible—the same Bible which prophecies about Jesus, the Savior who would come to save mankind. However, these people ultimately fell under Satan's control and nailed Jesus to the cross. They proclaimed they served God and boasted about their knowledge of the Law. Yet without cultivating their hearts with the truth, they killed the Messiah for whom they had waited for so long. These people continued in their ways as they also persecuted the disciples who testified about Jesus' resurrection. It was as it was written, "All these things they will do to you for My name's sake."

So why did the people claim to believe in God but end up being hostile towards Him? It was because they did not know God's heart, love, will, or providence for sending Jesus into this world. They were so obsessed with the Law and their own self-righteousness that they incorporated their fleshly thoughts into everything they did, and saw everything with that same perspective. It is no wonder that the actions they took were far from displaying God's love.

If Jesus had not shared the word of life with people like the Pharisees, the Sadducees, and the high priests; and if 'signs' had not confirmed His words, then they would not have committed the evil act of judging, condemning, and persecuting Jesus. But because Jesus, who is Light, shone with God's Word, their dark and evil ways were discovered. They had no excuse for their sins.

Hating Jesus is the same as hating God. If someone truly believes in God, he should be able to recognize Jesus, who was sent into this world by God. And as Jesus said, "But now they have both seen...Me and My Father," Jesus showed God to them through the signs He performed.

However, they judged Jesus' every move with their traditions, and acted in collusion with their fleshly thoughts to find fault in Him. They not only refused to believe in Him; but they also hated and ostracized Him. Therefore we cannot say they are without sin. The fact that they ostracized Jesus because of their fleshly thoughts is evidence that they hated not only Jesus, but also God who sent Him.

Concerning their actions, Jesus said it was fulfillment of the Scriptures that state there are many who hated Him without a cause (Psalm 35:19, 69:4). From this we can learn that God's every word is fulfilled without error, and that we should believe in His Word from the very center of our hearts. We should strive to equip ourselves with God's Word; but not by piling up mere head-knowledge, like the Pharisees, but by cultivating our hearts with the truth.

"When the Helper comes, whom I will send to you from the Father, that is the Spirit of truth who proceeds from the Father, He will testify about Me, and you will testify also, because you have been with Me from the beginning" (15:26-27).

This passage is about the role of the Holy Spirit, who was to come after Jesus died on the cross and completely fulfilled His calling. The Holy Spirit, or the Helper, testifies about who Jesus is. By spreading the truth that Jesus is the Savior, He leads many people on towards salvation.

In actuality, 10 days after Jesus ascended into Heaven, the Holy Spirit came upon the people who believed in Jesus' promise and who were gathered together to pray. The disciples of Jesus who received the Holy Spirit began to lead lives that were very different from before. Just as Jesus said, "You will testify also, because you have been with Me from the beginning," with the power of the Holy Spirit, they took on their calling as true witnesses. Jesus knew about the works of the Holy Spirit that would occur, and He also knew what kind of ministry the disciples would be taking on. Jesus told His disciples about these future events because He wanted His disciples to receive the Holy Spirit and well fulfill their calling as His witnesses.

Chapter 16

The Helper, Holy Spirit

1. The Coming and Ministry of the Holy Spirit
(16:1-15)

2. The Prophecy of Jesus' Death and Resurrection
(16:16-24)

3. Jesus, Who Had Victory Over the World
(16:25-33)

The Coming and Ministry of the Holy Spirit

After finishing the Passover meal and comforting the disciples and giving them several more lessons, Jesus began teaching about the work of the Holy Spirit. He told them that the Holy Spirit would come to convict and rebuke the world concerning sin, righteousness, and judgment. Also, not only would He lead the disciples to the way of truth; but He would also let them know about the events to come in the future.

The Condition of Jesus' Heart As He Told His Disciples About Future Events

"These things I have spoken to you so that you may be kept from stumbling. They will make you outcasts from the synagogue, but an hour is coming for everyone who kills you to think that he is offering service to God. These things they will do because they have not known the Father or Me. But these things I have spoken to you, so that when their hour comes, you may remember that I told you of them. These things I did not say to you at the beginning, because I was with you" (16:1-4).

Jesus first revealed why He was telling the disciples about the events to come. He did not want any one of them to become discouraged and give up their faith when Jesus takes up the cross, or when they experience suffering. From God's perspective, Jesus' suffering was permitted by Him for the salvation of mankind; by no means was it because Jesus had no power. Because it was permitted under God's providence for mankind's salvation, evildoers were able to persecute Him.

The evil people did not know that God was allowing Jesus to suffer and die on the cross so He can gain one of the qualifications to become the Savior. They simply thought they were killing Jesus by their own power and authority. In addition, they thought Jesus' words were blaspheming God; so they believed that killing Jesus was carrying out their ultimate duty before God. Therefore, Jesus told them once again why He was telling them about the ordeal that lay ahead.

"But these things I have spoken to you, so that when their hour comes, you may remember that I told you of them.

These things I did not say to you at the beginning, because I was with you."

This shows how precise and timely Jesus was, with everything He said and did. If Jesus had told them in the very beginning that He would be taking up the cross and that all these events would occur, the disciples probably would have had a hard time gaining true faith. They needed to pass through the coming trials with their own faith in order for their faith to be acknowledged as true faith. Just as an exam cannot be a good evaluation if the answer key has already been disclosed, no matter how much Jesus loved His disciples, He had to let them take on their own tests in a fair manner. This is why Jesus waited patiently until after Judas Iscariot left to turn Him over to the officials before He told all these things to the remaining disciples.

"It Is to Your Advantage That I Go Away"

"But now I am going to Him who sent Me; and none of you asks Me, 'Where are You going?' But because I have said these things to you, sorrow has filled your heart. But I tell you the truth, it is to your advantage that I go away; for if I do not go away, the Helper will not come to you; but if I go, I will send Him to you" (16:5-7).

After Jesus told them He was leaving, the disciples became anxious and worried. But not a single one of them would ask where He was going. While they were with Jesus, witnessing God's works, their hearts were confident and bold. At that time, they felt like they had faith, and they thought they understood all of Jesus' words. However, now that they learned that Jesus was leaving, their hearts were troubled.

So Jesus told these concerned disciples about how beneficial it will be when the Holy Spirit comes. He told them that if He does not leave, the Helper cannot come; and therefore it is better for them that He leaves. Once the disciples receive the Holy Spirit, they would come to understand God's love as He fulfilled the providence of salvation by sending His one and only Son into this world. Jesus gave the disciples comfort and hope as He explained that once they receive the Holy Spirit they would be empowered by God's great love and thereby gain a strong platform of true faith.

The Work of Our Helper the Holy Spirit

"And He, when He comes, will convict the world concerning sin and righteousness and judgment; concerning sin, because they do not believe in Me; and concerning righteousness, because I go to the Father and you no longer see Me; and concerning judgment, because the ruler of this world has been judged. I have many more things to say to you, but you cannot bear them now" (16:8-12).

Jesus told the disciples what kind of work the Helper, or the

Holy Spirit would do once He comes. He explained that the Holy Spirit would convict the world about sin, righteousness, and judgment, and ring the alarming bell for all people to hear.

"Concerning sin, because they do not believe in Me..."
When Jesus said this, He meant that when we receive the Holy Spirit, we realize that we are sinners, and that Jesus died to save us from sin. Also, with the help of the Holy Spirit, we come to understand the great love of God, which caused Him to give up His one and only Son. And finally, we also become convicted that not knowing God was a sin, and therefore repent.

Jesus continued to say, "And concerning righteousness, because I go to the Father and you no longer see Me..." After dying on the cross, Jesus resurrected, and went to God the Father. In Romans 5:18 it says, *So then as through one transgression there resulted condemnation to all men, even so through one act of righteousness there resulted justification of life to all men.*" When we receive the Holy Spirit, we are able to believe in Jesus' 'one act of righteousness', which is the providence of salvation by the cross. And all those who believe in this, God acknowledges as 'righteous'.

If we truly believe in the fact that Jesus died upon the cross for us, we will certainly keep God's Word; and as much as we live according His Word, we become one with the Lord. This is why God recognizes us as righteous. Therefore, since we have been called righteous by the Lord's grace, if we keep God's Word with true faith and live accordingly, we can cast out the evil from our hearts and become sanctified. This is because the Holy Spirit guides the children of God to the way of truth so that they can become righteous people.

Lastly, Jesus said, "And concerning judgment, because the ruler of this world has been judged..." Here, 'ruler of this world' signifies the enemy devil and Satan. What Jesus meant by this is that the Holy Spirit will help us know that the enemy devil and Satan have already received judgment.

When Adam and Eve fell into Satan's temptation and committed the sin of disobeying God's Word, their descendants became slaves to sin; and because of the spiritual law that says the penalty of sin is death, they began going to the way of death. But along came the enemy Satan, who by killing Jesus, broke the spiritual law because Jesus had no sin. Therefore, death no longer has authority over those who believe in Jesus Christ. This is why in Romans 8:2 it says, *"For the law of the Spirit of life in Christ Jesus has set you free from the law of sin and of death."*

So the Holy Spirit helps us know that the enemy devil and Satan have received judgment; meaning they cannot lead believers in Christ to death. "The ruler of this world has been judged" also means that at the Judgment of the White Throne, the enemy devil and Satan will receive eternal judgment. Of course the disciples could not understand all these things at the time; but, when the Holy Spirit comes, they would remember all of Jesus' words and understand each word.

When the Spirit of Truth Comes

"But when He, the Spirit of truth, comes, He will guide you into all the truth; for He will not speak on His own initiative, but whatever He hears, He will speak; and He will disclose to you what is to come. He will glorify Me, for He will take of Mine and will disclose it to you. All things that the Father has are Mine; therefore I said that He takes of Mine and will disclose it to you" (16:13-15).

Jesus continued to teach the disciples about the ministry of the Holy Spirit. He called Him the "Spirit of Truth" and said, "He will guide you into all the truth." This is because the Holy Spirit is one with God at heart and guides us into the truth. When the Holy Spirit comes, He gives us the grace to break away our flesh thoughts and gives us more power to understand the deep heart of God (1 Corinthians 2:10). Also, He will never speak out of His own will, but will speak only what He hears and let us know about the events to come in the future. He speaks only in accordance with God's will.

"He will glorify Me, for He will take of Mine and will disclose it to you. All things that the Father has are Mine."

Here we can see that Jesus, the Holy Spirit, and God are completely one. The heart of Jesus is the heart of the Holy Spirit, and the heart of the Holy Spirit is the heart of Jesus. By origin They are one, but for the providence of the cultivation of man, They took on different roles.

What the Holy Spirit says is what Jesus is saying, and the word of Jesus is the Word of God. Therefore when the Holy Spirit comes He teaches about Jesus, and when powerful works are done in Jesus Christ's name, God is glorified; but God is sharing this glory with the Lord Jesus and the Holy Spirit.

The Prophecy of Jesus' Death and Resurrection

Jesus not only showed numerous evidences to the disciples so they could believe, but He also told them about the events to come in the future. He told them about how Judas Iscariot would sell Him, about how He would be captured by the Jews when He went up to Jerusalem, and about how He would die on the cross and come back to life on the third day. Even after hearing these words, the disciples could not understand.

The Disciples Do Not Understand the Spiritual Message

"'A little while, and you will no longer see Me; and again a little while, and you will see Me.' Some of His disciples then said to one another, 'What is this thing He is telling us, "A little while, and you will not see Me; and again a little while, and you will see Me"; and, "because I go to the Father"?' So they were saying, 'What is this that He says, "A little while"? We do not know what He is talking about.' Jesus knew that they wished to question Him, and He said to them, 'Are you deliberating together about this, that I said, "A little while, and you will not see Me, and again a little while, and you will see Me"?'" (16:16-19).

When Jesus completes His mission and goes up to Heaven, He would no longer be with the disciples. This is why He said, "A little while, and you will no longer see Me." But when the Holy Spirit—who is one with Jesus—comes, they would be able to meet again. At that time, the disciples could not understand how the Holy Spirit's coming meant they could be with Jesus again.

Jesus knew the disciples would not understand, but the reason He said these things was because He knew that later when the Holy Spirit came upon them, they would understand the spiritual meaning of His words and put their lives on the line to work for the kingdom of God. In actuality, after receiving the Holy Spirit, the disciples were totally transformed, and they sacrificed their whole lives for the work of spreading the gospel of Jesus Christ. And most of them were even martyred for the cause. However, when they heard these words from Jesus, they hadn't received the Holy Spirit yet, and therefore they were very confused.

"What is this that He says, 'A little while'? We do not know what He is talking about." Jesus pinpoints exactly what the disciples' question was: "Are you deliberating together about this, that I said, 'A little while, and you will not see Me, and again a little while, and you will see Me'?"

Jesus used the words "A little while" in order to explain the events that were about to occur in the future. However, the disciples, limited by their fleshly thoughts, tried to confine these words to a secular definition. When Jesus said, "A little while, and you will see Me," the spiritual meaning of these words means that when the Holy Spirit comes, they will be able to see Jesus because Jesus and the Holy Spirit are one; but it also means that Jesus will resurrect in three days and actually physically appear before the disciples.

In Corinthians 15:4-6, it says that *"... and that He [Jesus] was buried, and that He was raised on the third day according to the Scriptures, and that He appeared to Cephas, then to the twelve. After that He appeared to more than five hundred brethren at one time."*

"Your Grief Will Be Turned Into Joy"

"Truly, truly, I say to you, that you will weep and lament, but the world will rejoice; you will grieve, but your grief will be turned into joy. Whenever a woman is in labor she has pain, because her hour has come; but when she gives birth to the child, she no longer remembers the anguish because of the joy that a child has been born into the world. Therefore you too have grief now; but I will see you again, and your heart will rejoice, and no one will take your joy away from you" (16:20-22).

Because Jesus was saying, 'I am leaving. In a little while you will no longer see Me,' the disciples felt as though the skies were falling down upon them. Knowing what was going on in their hearts, Jesus said: "You will weep and lament, but the world will rejoice; you will grieve, but your grief will be turned into joy." Here we can see the difference between perceiving a certain situation with fleshly eyes, and seeing the same situation with spiritual eyes. Let's take Jesus' suffering for example. When we perceive and understand this event with spiritual eyes, we know that this is something we should be joyful about. However, when we look at this same event with fleshly eyes, it is a very sad event, and for the disciples, it was an unimaginable tragedy. This is why Jesus said, "You will weep and lament." But He also added, "But the world will rejoice." What does this mean?

Here, the "world" signifies mankind that had to become slaves of the enemy devil because of the curse they received because of sin. Through Adam's sin, all of his descendants received the curse of *"The wages of sin is death"* (Romans 6:23). However, Jesus redeemed all mankind from their sins, destroyed the enemy devil and Satan's power over death, and opened up the way to eternal life. How can one not be joyful?

Once the disciples received the Holy Spirit, they would clearly understand this providence of God. That is why Jesus said, "You will grieve, but your grief will be turned into joy."

Then He used this illustration, "Whenever a woman is in labor she has pain, because her hour has come; but when she gives birth to the child, she no longer remembers the anguish because of the joy that a child has been born into the world." When it is time for a woman to give birth, she experiences great pain. But the moment she holds her child in her bosom, she forgets about all the pain she suffered because the child is so precious and lovely.

Furthermore, Jesus said, "I will see you again, and your heart will rejoice, and no one will take your joy away from you." When Jesus told the disciples "I will see you again", He was referring to the fact that they would actually get to see Him in person, after His resurrection, and the fact that they would later receive the Holy Spirit. He was explaining that once they see the resurrected Jesus and receive the Holy Spirit in their hearts, they would be full of joy. This joy comes from the true peace and faith that comes from God, therefore no one can take this joy away. Jesus repeatedly told the disciples this truth, which shows His unwavering determination to fully take on the mission of completing the providence of salvation through the cross. This was because no matter how the enemy devil and Satan tried to interfere using all kinds of evil schemes and connivances, the salvation through the cross would be completed and Jesus would resurrect overcoming death in the midst of God's astounding wisdom.

Ask In the Name of Jesus Christ

"In that day you will not question Me about anything. Truly, truly, I say to you, if you ask the Father for anything in My name, He will give it to you. Until now you have asked for nothing in My name; ask and you will receive, so that your joy may be made full" (16:23-24).

Here, "In that day" refers to the time after the disciples receive the Holy Spirit. When the Holy Spirit dwells in each person's heart, He helps that person remember Jesus' words and helps him understand the meaning of those words. Now, because of the Holy Spirit, we can understand things that we otherwise could not have understood on our own, and we can become enlightened about all kinds of things that we might have had questions about before. We can also feel God's love and even understand His amazing providence.

"Truly, truly, I say to you, if you ask the Father for anything in My name, He will give it to you. Until now you have asked for nothing in My name; ask and you will receive, so that your joy may be made full."

What can we learn from this verse? First, we learn that there is great power in the name of Jesus Christ. Because God is so pleased with Jesus for completely fulfilling His calling as the Savior, to anyone who asks in His name, God answers his prayers.

However, there is a difference in the power when we pray

in the name of "Jesus", and when we pray in the name of "Jesus Christ". As it is written in Matthew 1:21, "Jesus" means *"He will save His people from their sins."* So "Jesus" does not mean "He who saved", in the past tense, but "He who will save" in the future tense. On the other hand, "Christ" means "The Anointed One", which signifies "The Peacemaker between God and man, the Savior, and the Mediator." So the name "Jesus Christ" carries in it the meaning, "Jesus completed and fulfilled His calling as the Savior."

Therefore it is not when we pray in the name of "Jesus", but when we pray in the name of "Jesus Christ", that we experience the power. Jesus came to this world according to God's will, and He humbled Himself and submitted to the point of dying on the cross. And, because God was so pleased with the fact that in all things Jesus answered with 'Yes' and 'Amen', He happily answers when anyone asks in this name of Jesus Christ.

Next, we can also learn the difference between thoughts of the spirit and thoughts of the flesh. From the disciples' perspective, Jesus' dreadful death on the cross was a very painful and mournful event. But through the providence of the cross, the curse upon mankind turned into a blessing, and now with the power in the name of Jesus Christ, we can easily defeat the enemy devil and Satan! So from a spiritual perspective, this was a rather joyful event.

Finally, through this verse, we can feel the gentle and thorough love of Jesus. Before taking up the cross, Jesus told the disciples about His death, resurrection, ascension, and the coming Holy Spirit in order to help them prepare their hearts for what is to come. Even though they did not completely understand at the time, He wanted to make sure that in the future they would realize the complete plan and providence of God and come to the point of sacrificing their lives to fulfill their callings. The disciples would constantly be reminded of such love of the Lord so that they would not fall into despair but win the victory in any persecution.

Jesus, Who Had Victory Over the World

In the Four Gospels, there are an especially large number of parables. There is the parable of the sower, the parable of the talents, the parable of the prodigal son, the parable of the farmer of the vineyard, the parable of the grape vine and branches, the parable of the mustard seed, etc. A parable uses everyday things that people encounter in order to tell some meaning or lesson in an easy way for people to understand, and it also has the effect of not blatantly giving away the intent or motive of the person telling the parable.

For example, when Jesus told the people that He would destroy the temple and then rebuild it in three days, He was using a parable to tell them about His death and resurrection. The reason Jesus spoke using parables was because not only is it hard to explain about the spiritual world with the language of this world; but it is also hard to comprehend spiritual things with mere human knowledge.

An Hour Is Coming When I Will Tell You Plainly

"These things I have spoken to you in figurative language; an hour is coming when I will no longer speak to you in figurative language, but will tell you plainly of the Father. In that day you will ask in My name, and I do not say to you that I will request of the Father on your behalf; for the Father Himself loves you, because you have loved Me and have believed that I came forth from the Father" (16:25-27).

Up to this point, in consideration of His disciples who could not clearly understand the spiritual realm, Jesus used the various parables to help them understand. However, there is a limit to how much one can explain the infinite and vast spiritual world using illustrations from things of this world. That is why Jesus said, "An hour is coming when I will no longer speak to you in figurative language, but will tell you plainly of the Father." Here, "An hour" refers to the advent of the Holy Spirit.

At the time, the disciples could not understand why Jesus had to take up the cross, and how God would be glorified; even if Jesus was to explain to them in parables. But when the Holy Spirit teaches them later on, they would be able to understand fully.

Surely after Jesus' resurrection and ascension, when the

disciples received the Holy Spirit, they came to realize God's providence. As a fisherman in the past, Peter had very little education, but after receiving the Holy Spirit, he was able to speak aptly and without hesitation about the true meaning of God's words contained in the laws (Acts chapter 3). Since he was being taught by the Holy Spirit, who understands even the deep heart of God, the Creator of the universe, Peter was not bound by any limitations.

On top of that, as Jesus said, "In that day you will ask in My name," whenever the disciples asked in the name of Jesus Christ, God's power was shown. In Acts 3:6, we see Peter saying to a lame beggar, *"I do not possess silver and gold, but what I do have I give to you: In the name of Jesus Christ the Nazarene—walk!"* At that very moment, strength came into the beggar's feet and ankles, and he began to walk and leap and praise God.

The reason why our prayers are answered when we pray in the name of Jesus Christ is because God is greatly pleased by that name; but it is also because He is pleased by the faith we show when we believe in His name and thereby seek in His name. This action shows God that we acknowledge and have faith in the fact that He sent His only begotten Son, Jesus, into this world, and it also shows Him that we acknowledge and have faith in the fact that everything Jesus Christ did, including His death on the cross, His resurrection, and His ascension, was all part of God's plan and providence.

When Jesus said, "You have loved Me and have believed that I came forth from the Father," Jesus was talking about having faith in the fact that Jesus—who is by origin, one with God—is the only Son who came into this world in the flesh. When we love Jesus and we depend on His name when we pray, God considers that faith, and He answers us. Of course those who love the Son whom He sent, and those who obey His Son's words receive God's love!

> **"'I came forth from the Father and have come into the world; I am leaving the world again and going to the Father.' His disciples said, 'Lo, now You are speaking plainly and are not using a figure of speech. Now we know that You know all things, and have no need for anyone to question You; by this we believe that You came from God'" (16:28-30).**

When it came close to the time that He had to take up the cross, He clearly disclosed who He was—not only who He was by origin, but how He was acting in accordance with God's providence, and what events would take place later on. He wanted the disciples to inscribe into their hearts what they talked about that night, and never to forget it.

Jesus was not just looking at how the disciples were at that time. Because He was seeing how they would be after their transformation later on, He wanted to give them words of love, encouragement, and hope until the very end (Luke 22:28-32). That is when the disciples finally made their confession of faith. Although they did not have complete faith yet, because Jesus spoke to them with such love and compassion, they acknowledged with their hearts and confessed with their lips.

"Take Courage; I Have Overcome the World"

"Jesus answered them, 'Do you now believe? Behold, an hour is coming, and has already come, for you to be scattered, each to his own home, and to leave Me alone; and yet I am not alone, because the Father is with Me. These things I have spoken to you, so that in Me you may have peace. In the world you have tribulation, but take courage; I have overcome the world'" (16:31-33).

To the disciples who tried to make their confessions of faith, Jesus asked once again, "Do you now believe?"

Jesus saw right into their hearts. He told them what they would do while He was taking on the suffering. However, He was not telling them this to scorn them for not being able to fight and for not overcoming their fears and fleeing away from their teacher. He wanted them to know that even though they leave, He will not be alone because in spirit, He would be with God.

Because all these things were part of God's plan and providence, even if everyone left and He was left alone, Jesus was saying even *that* is part of His responsibility.

Even though they spent a long time with Jesus, and they felt the truth with their hearts, because of their fleshly thoughts, the disciples could not have complete faith. For that reason each of them was in anguish. Especially Peter, who confessed in Matthew 16:16, *"You are the Christ, the Son of the living God,"* ultimately denied Jesus three times. So how emotionally distressed do you think he was?

This anguish that the disciples felt because of their inability to have complete faith, was what Jesus was referring to when He said, "In the world you have tribulation." He also said this to signify the persecution and all the different types of hardship the disciples would later face as they go around to preach about Jesus Christ. However, when one receives persecution for the name of Jesus Christ, spiritually it is considered a reward; and in Heaven, it is a compliment and a glory.

Jesus' disciples were not facing tribulation because God does not have power; the trials and sufferings were all part of God's providence being carried out in the midst of His complete love and justice. That is why Jesus said, "Take courage; I have overcome the world."

Sure enough, Jesus died on the cross, had victory over death, resurrected, and became the true Savior. So as much as we are one with Jesus in faith, that's how much we can have victory in this world through His name. When we have spiritual faith, we can destroy the stronghold of the enemy devil and Satan and boldly preach about God's glory.

Chapter 17

Jesus' Intercessory Prayer

1. A Prayer for Taking Up the Cross
(17:1-5)

2. A Prayer for the Disciples
(17:6-19)

3. A Prayer for the Believers
(17:20-26)

A Prayer for Taking Up the Cross

As God's Word is the bread of life, prayer is the breath of one's spirit. Even Jesus lifted up many prayers while He was here on earth. He habitually went up to the Mount of Olives to pray. He also sought quiet places like the Garden of Gethsemane to pray. He prayed at the Jordan River, and He even prayed on the cross. And just before His suffering on the cross, He prayed so earnestly that His sweat became like drops of blood (Luke 22:44).

Just before He was arrested by the soldiers sent by the high priests and the Pharisees, Jesus prayed a very earnest prayer to God. Even though He is God's Son, in accordance with the words, *"Ask, and it will be given to you,"* Jesus set a model for prayer (Matthew 7:7).

Jesus Saw the Glory to Come

"Jesus spoke these things; and lifting up His eyes to heaven, He said, 'Father, the hour has come; glorify Your Son, that the Son may glorify You'" (17:1).

After comforting His disciples, Jesus knew it was time for Him to fulfill His calling as the Savior. But instead of thinking about the suffering that He would soon face, He saw the glory that would come after the suffering. No matter what kind of suffering He faced, He had assurance of seeing the glory after that. He knew that His death on the cross was not the result of man's thoughts or plans, but that it was part of God's providence.

When Jesus prayed, "Father, the hour has come; glorify Your Son," He was saying, "It is time. Allow me to be captured by men and to be nailed to the cross." On several occasions up until this point, the enemy devil and Satan had incited people who were to kill Jesus, but it was not yet time, so God did not allow this to happen. But now, the time had come.

The execution on the cross seems appalling to the physical eye, but Jesus knew that that was the way to glory. After He destroyed the power of death, resurrected, and completed His calling as the Savior, He would receive the spiritual honor and glory of becoming the King of Kings, and the Lord of Lords. So when Jesus prayed, "Glorify Your Son, that the Son may glorify You," He was saying that He lifts up to God all the glory He will receive after His suffering on the cross. These words were also an expression of Jesus' love for God, showing His desire to glorify God by faithfully fulfilling His calling as the Savior.

> **"Even as You gave Him authority over all flesh, that to all whom You have given Him, He may give eternal life. This is eternal life, that they may know You, the only true God, and Jesus Christ whom You have sent"** (17:2-3).

So after the suffering on the cross, what kind of glory did God and Jesus receive? By sending His only begotten Son Jesus into this world and allowing Him to die on the cross, God received countless children of faith. And after that, He *"Bestowed on Him [Jesus] the name which is above every name,"* and gave His Son the supreme authority over all things (Philippians 2:9-11).

God originally gave this authority to the first man, Adam. But as a result of taking and eating the fruit of knowledge of good and evil, Adam became a slave to sin, handing over all authority to the enemy devil and Satan.

In Luke 4:5-7, after Jesus finished His 40 days of fasting, the devil came to Him and showed Him all the kingdoms of the world. Then he tempted Jesus, saying, *"I will give You all this domain and its glory; for it has been handed over to me, and I give it to whomever I wish. Therefore if You worship before me, it shall all be Yours."*

According to the word which states that you become slaves to whom you obey, if you worship the devil, you become his slave (Romans 6:16). Knowing the devil's wicked scheme, Jesus firmly cast the temptation away by saying, *"It is written, 'YOU SHALL WORSHIP THE LORD YOUR GOD AND SERVE HIM ONLY'"* (Luke 4:8).

The enemy devil and Satan gained power by connivingly deceiving Adam and Eve. However, Jesus attempted to redeem that power while strictly adhering to the spiritual law. By sacrificing Himself completely, He redeemed that power from the devil.

When we believe in this Jesus, we can defeat and subdue the enemy devil and Satan. We can have protection against temptations and tribulations, illnesses and accidents. Not only that, we gain eternal life, so instead of going to eternal death, or Hell, we go to Heaven eternal.

Then what does it mean when the Scripture says "Knowing God and Jesus Christ is eternal life"? John 6:40 says, *"For this is the will of My Father, that everyone who beholds the Son and believes in Him will have eternal life, and I Myself will raise him up on the last day."*

God sent His Son into this world so that all peoples can receive salvation. By allowing Jesus—who was sinless, and who was goodness and love itself—to be nailed to the cross, God made Him the Savior of many people. Therefore man, who rightfully has to go to Hell because of sin, can gain eternal life by believing in Jesus Christ.

Those people who gained salvation through Jesus Christ come to know very well about how God poured out such love to the undeserving sinners. They come to know the truth about God—not a scary God who judges strictly according to the

Law—but a God of love, who sacrificed His own Son in order to make a way of salvation for the sinners. Therefore, those who experienced the true joy of salvation know that there is nothing greater than the grace of Jesus Christ and the love of God; so they call God "Abba Father".

"Father, Glorify Me together with Yourself"

"I glorified You on the earth, having accomplished the work which You have given Me to do. Now, Father, glorify Me together with Yourself, with the glory which I had with You before the world was" (17:4-5).

Jesus glorified God by fulfilling all of God's plan and providence, so He lifted up a prayer asking God to glorify Him as well. Jesus was originally one with God before the creation and the glory that He had was so noble and beautiful that it cannot be explained with human words. But in order to fulfill God's will, He put all this glory behind Him, put on the flesh, and came into this world and took upon the death on the cross to complete His calling as the Savior.

As it is written in 1 Corinthians 10:31, *"Whether, then, you eat or drink or whatever you do, do all to the glory of God,"* during His ministry here on earth, Jesus never sought for His own riches or fame. He only sought to glorify God. Therefore He could boldly pray, "Father, glorify Me together with Yourself."

God wants us, like Jesus, to glorify God in everything that

we do. This is not because God wants to receive all the glory. According to the spiritual law which says one shall reap what he sows, God wants to give each of us the reward and glory that is fitting of a child of His. That is why in John 13:32, Jesus said, *"If God is glorified in Him, God will also glorify Him in Himself, and will glorify Him immediately."*

A Prayer for the Disciples

In order to complete God's work, Jesus rarely had time to rest or sleep. Regardless, He never ceased praying. Now that it was time for Him to carry out the ministry of the cross, how much more earnestly He must have prayed! First He prayed that He might glorify God, and then He prayed for His loving disciples.

Jesus Saw His Disciples with Faith

"I have manifested Your name to the men whom You gave Me out of the world; they were Yours and You gave them to Me, and they have kept Your word" (17:6).

When Jesus said, "I have manifested Your name," He meant that He taught about God's heart and will. Jesus was with God before the creation, and He created the universe with God. So of course He was able to clearly show God's heart and will.

Jesus said, "They were Yours and You gave them to Me, and they have kept Your word." Here, 'they' refer to the people who are being cultivated by God so as to become His true children. They belong to God, but Jesus said, "You gave them to Me," because they gain salvation through Him, Jesus Christ. And when referring to those people who are saved, Jesus confessed, "...and they have kept Your word." This means that they truly believe in God and have accepted Jesus as their Savior; therefore they have the qualification to be saved.

As it is written in James 2:22, *"You see that faith was working with his works, and as a result of the works, faith was perfected,"* true faith is followed by actions. The fact that they 'kept God's Word' means that they have the faith to be saved, or the faith to act according to God's Word.

"Now they have come to know that everything You have given Me is from You; for the words which You gave Me I have given to them; and they received them and truly understood that I came forth from You, and they believed that You sent Me" (17:7-8).

If a person believes that the powerful works of Jesus are of God, he will also believe that Jesus is the Savior. As one is able to recognize the tree by its fruit, if one performs signs and wonders, we can recognize that God is with him. Jesus was telling God about the disciples and other people who had this pure kind of faith. This does not mean that these people had complete faith at this time. It means that with goodness, they confessed and believed in God and Jesus from the deepest part of their hearts.

So Jesus was praying for God's mercy to be with the disciples and the good people who, even though they were still weak, had faith embedded within good hearts. Jesus knew the faith of His disciples very well. Even though they would all flee in fear when Jesus was captured (Matthew 26:31), Jesus prayed, picturing how they would later gain complete faith and transform into the Lord's powerful witnesses. Through this prayer, we can see Jesus' true love. Even though He saw 99 negative factors, He just told God about the one positive factor He saw.

> **"I ask on their behalf; I do not ask on behalf of the world, but of those whom You have given Me; for they are Yours; and all things that are Mine are Yours, and Yours are Mine; and I have been glorified in them"** (17:9-10).

"The world" here signifies the enemy devil and Satan who stand in opposition to Jesus Christ. God of love did send Jesus into this world to save all mankind; but this does not mean everyone will be saved. A person whose heart is evil, and who gives control of himself over to Satan ultimately will not be saved. The word of life and eternal life is for those people who believe in Jesus as their Savior; and it was for these people whom Jesus prayed to God for.

"All things that are Mine are Yours, and Yours are Mine," shows how God and Jesus are one (1 Corinthians 8:6). This means that because the Two are one, the glory and the suffering that Jesus received, God also received. Furthermore, the glory that Jesus would receive after dying on the cross, resurrecting, and becoming the Savior, God would also receive.

Jesus knew that through His suffering on the cross, the door to salvation would be opened; and that many souls would believe in the Lord and become true children of God. He also made this confession because He knew that these souls will give glory to God, who, out of His amazing love, prepared the way of salvation, and to Jesus Christ, who sacrificed Himself completely in order to fulfill God's will.

"That They May Be One Even As We Are"

"I am no longer in the world; and yet they themselves are in the world, and I come to You. Holy Father, keep them in Your name, the name which You have given Me, that they may be one even as We are" (17:11).

How can we ever completely express Jesus' affection for His disciples? Because He had to leave behind the ones He loved so much, He prayed, and prayed again to the Father God on their behalf. Jesus was leaving, but soon after, the Holy Spirit, whom He promised, would be coming. A person who believes in, and obeys the word of truth that the Holy Spirit teaches, that person can become one with God, as Jesus and God are one.

Up to this point, the disciples learned the truth from Jesus, and when they obeyed His words, they experienced amazing things (Matthew 17:27). When the Holy Spirit comes, everyone would see more amazing works of God, just like the times when Jesus was actually here on earth. Moreover, when Jesus was here, one had to be near Him to hear the word of truth, but when the Holy Spirit comes upon each individual person, anyone can hear the word of truth and receive God's command at any time. That is why Jesus prayed asking God to pour the Holy Spirit upon His beloved disciples so they may successfully fulfill God's will.

> **"While I was with them, I was keeping them in Your name which You have given Me; and I guarded them and not one of them perished but the son of perdition, so that the Scripture would be fulfilled" (17:12-13).**

When Jesus said, "I was keeping them in Your name," He meant that He cared for them with God's heart and love. Jesus came into this world in the name of God. He taught with words of authority, and by showing miraculous power, He led His disciples to live in the truth. However, there were exceptions. As Jesus said, "Not one of them perished but the son of perdition, so that the Scripture would be fulfilled," Judas Iscariot ultimately betrayed Him and went to the way of death.

This did not happen because Jesus lacked power—it was an event that was already prophesied in the Bible. It happened just as it is written in Psalm 41:9, *"Even my close friend in whom I trusted, who ate my bread, has lifted up his heel against me."* In appearance, it seems like Jesus was captured because of Judas Iscariot, but all things occurred because it was permitted by God.

Jesus taking up the cross does not show that the enemy devil and Satan had victory—it shows that God's plan of salvation for mankind followed through without fail. This also shows God's consideration for the disciples so that later on, they do not lose strength, but rather feel joy as they experience the work of the Holy Spirit.

"I have given them Your word; and the world has hated them, because they are not of the world, even as I am not of the world" (17:14).

The words that Jesus gave to His disciples were the truth and the light itself. But the world, or the people who are part of the enemy devil and Satan, hated Jesus, who was the Light (John 3:20). After listening to Jesus' words, the high priests and the Pharisees, instead of repenting, were eager to kill Jesus (Matthew chapter 21). The world also hated the disciples, who were part of the Light, because they received God's Word from Jesus, who was the Light.

In John 15:19 Jesus said, *"If you were of the world, the world would love its own; but because you are not of the world, but I chose you out of the world, because of this the world hates you."* Like this, if we don't partner up with this world, we are bound to be hated by it. In Matthew 10:35-36, it is written, *"For I came to set a man against his father, and a daughter against her mother, and a daughter-in-law against her mother-in-law; and a man's enemies will be the members of his household."* This means that at times, when we act in the truth, our own family members, who are not believers, may not understand us and even come to dislike us.

However, a person who loves the Lord and knows the truth will not become one with the world, even if it means experiencing hardship. If a person is not of the truth a true believer will not compromise with him, even if the person is a family member. Therefore, a believer will not join hands with darkness. Just as light and darkness cannot mix, if anyone loves the world or the things of the world, God's love is not in him. Jesus told the disciples in detail all the events that they would experience in the near future, as they happily take on the calling of being the Lord's witnesses. Then once again He lifted up an earnest prayer entrusting His disciples to God.

"I do not ask You to take them out of the world, but to keep them from the evil one" (17:15).

Some parents over-protect their children like plants in a greenhouse, and they raise them to become dependent people. But wise parents equip their children with the ability to face adversity on their own. Instead of catching the fish for them, they teach them how to catch the fish.

God's heart is the same way. He cultivates us so that we can fight evil with good and become children who take after God's own image. Knowing God's heart, Jesus did not pray asking God to take His disciples from this sinful world into Heaven; but to protect them from falling into sin. On one part, Jesus was alluding to the fact that after He left, the disciples would be able to live in the truth by the power of the Holy Spirit.

"Sanctify Them In the Truth..."

"They are not of the world, even as I am not of the world. Sanctify them in the truth; Your word is truth" (17:16-17).

During Jesus' public ministry, the disciples were always with Him, listening to His messages of truth, and witnessing His very actions. Following in Jesus' footsteps, they kept their hearts with the truth, and did not compromise with the world. While ministering with them, Jesus strongly led His disciples in the truth. He especially had them set strict boundaries so they did not become tied down by fleshly passions or blood relations (Luke 9:59-62).

He did this because if a person is tossed back and forth because of their blood relationships, scholarly relationships, or childhood relationships, one cannot make impartial decisions, and he can end up compromising with untruth. In Mark 10:29-30, Jesus said, *"Truly I say to you, there is no one who has left house or brothers or sisters or mother or father or children or farms, for My sake and for the gospel's sake, but that he will receive a hundred times as much now in the present age, houses and brothers and sisters and mothers and children and farms, along with persecutions; and in the age to come, eternal life."*

However, this does not mean one should be cold and irresponsible to their family. It is only right to do our duties to serve our parents. But it means that only after we nail our fleshly love and selfishness completely upon the cross, can we truly love God first and foremost, and honor our parents as true, faithful children. An excellent example of this is King Asa, the third king of Judah, the southern kingdom.

King Asa loved God, and he led a vast religious reformation and strictly purged idolatry. When his mother, Queen Maacah committed idolatry, he even deposed his own mother. He was concerned that if he overlooked his mother's actions, then idolatry would become prevalent among his people once again. However, even though he deposed his mother, he probably served and honored her nonetheless. And through this experience, Maacah would have been greatly enlightened, and it probably gave her a great opportunity to repent before God. Truly honoring one's parents is leading their souls to salvation.

As it is written in 2 Timothy 2:4, *"No soldier in active service entangles himself in the affairs of everyday life, so that he may please the one who enlisted him as a soldier,"* our blood relations and physical ties should not become a distraction to God's work. The reason Jesus led His disciples so strongly in the truth was because they had to take on the great responsibility of witnessing that Jesus is the Christ. But before becoming powerful workers fulfilling their callings, He wanted them first and foremost, to become holy in the truth.

As Jesus prayed, "Sanctify them in the truth," He wanted them to first recuperate the image of God in themselves. God wants to build His kingdom through children who are clothed in holiness. As Hebrews 12:14 says, *"Pursue peace with all men, and the sanctification without which no one will see the Lord,"* we need to be completely sanctified without having even the image of evil to live close to the Lord's throne and to share eternal happiness and joy when we get to Heaven.

"As You sent Me into the world, I also have sent them into the world. For their sakes I sanctify Myself, that they themselves also may be sanctified in truth" (17:18-19).

God sent Jesus into this world in the midst of His plan of salvation for mankind. So Jesus came with the mission of being the Savior. Therefore the disciples who would remain after Him had the mission of being His witnesses. That is why Jesus said, "I also have sent them into the world." With deeper introspection, we can see that this expression is embedded with Jesus' earnest plea to the Father God to give strength to the disciples so they can guard their hearts to faithfully complete their calling.

If they truly knew Jesus' heart, the disciples would not consider their calling of spreading the gospel as a difficult task. Thinking about the glory they would later receive in Heaven, they would actually be able to take on the calling with joy and thanksgiving. In the church, when asked to take on a special calling, some people answer, "I cannot take the calling because I'm not competent enough." But this is a wrong mindset.

Before the almighty God, man's ability—great or small—has no meaning. What's important is who can truly believe in God and have the ability to pray earnestly enough to pull His power down to this earth and experience it. And in order to experience this power, one must become sanctified. That is, one must cultivate a holy heart.

When we look at Mark chapter 9, we can see that this is true. One day, a father who had a demon-possessed son came seeking Jesus. He had visited the disciples before, because of this problem, but to no avail. Because the disciples were not completely transformed by the truth yet, the demon did not budge at their word. But as soon as Jesus said, *"You deaf and mute spirit, I command you, come out of him and do not enter him again"* (v. 25), the demon cried out and then left the young man. So in the spiritual world, the more holy and sinless one is, the more power he or she can exert.

This is why Jesus prayed, "For their sakes I sanctify Myself, that they themselves also may be sanctified in truth," desiring for the disciples to become perfect (Matthew 5:48). However, Jesus did not just simply *tell* His disciples, "Be holy, be perfect," but He *showed* them. In everything He did, He was a model to them.

A Prayer for the Believers

When we read the Bible, we can see how differently God the Creator thinks, and how His creation, the people, think. Isaiah 55:8-9 reads, *"'For My thoughts are not your thoughts, nor are your ways My ways,' declares the LORD. 'For as the heavens are higher than the earth, so are My ways higher than your ways and My thoughts than your thoughts.'"* Therefore the disciples could not dare understand the heart and thoughts of Jesus, who is one with God. After praying for Himself and His disciples, Jesus then prayed for the many souls that would come to receive salvation through the ministry of the disciples. How can people even come close to perceiving this great love of Jesus?

So That the World May Believe That You Sent Me...

"I do not ask on behalf of these alone, but for those also who believe in Me through their word; that they may all be one; even as You, Father, are in Me and I in You, that they also may be in Us, so that the world may believe that You sent Me" (17:20-21).

Jesus is not the Savior of just a few exceptional people. That is why Jesus beseeched the disciples to go into all the world and spread the gospel to all peoples, as recorded in Mark 16:15, *"Go into all the world and preach the gospel to all creation,"* and in Matthew 28:19, *"Go therefore and make disciples of all the nations, baptizing them in the name of the Father and the Son and the Holy Spirit."* This calling of spreading the gospel wasn't just for the disciples. Anyone who believes in Jesus Christ and receives salvation has a calling to spread the word about the grace of salvation that was given to all for free.

The apostle Paul confessed, *"I am under obligation both to Greeks and to barbarians, both to the wise and to the foolish. So, for my part, I am eager to preach the gospel to you also who are in Rome"* (Romans 1:14-15). Just as he confessed, because he was so thankful for the priceless love he received, he worked for the cause of spreading the gospel with all of his life.

However, it does not mean everyone hears the gospel and receives salvation. Only those who truly believe from the center of their hearts that God sent Jesus into this world as the Savior can receive salvation. Just as God is in Jesus, and Jesus is in God, a person must be one with Jesus in truth and in spirit.

To those who believe in the good works of Jesus, and who recognize Jesus as the Son of God, God gives them the gift of the Holy Spirit. Once a person receives the Holy Spirit, his knowledge-based faith ultimately changes into spiritual faith. He comes to understand the words of Jesus, and he comes to realize the true love of God that was great enough to send His only begotten Son into this world. Of course, how fast a person comes to understand, and how efficiently he or she begins to live according to the Word depends on each person.

The magnitude of goodness and innocense of one's heart and the extent of his obedience to the voice of the Holy Spirit determine the pace of his spiritual growth and decide when he can reach the wholesome level of faith where he is one with the Lord. For this reason, He prayed that all men may not just receive salvation but become one with Him in truth and spirit so that they would reach the wholesome level of faith.

> **"The glory which You have given Me I have given to them, that they may be one, just as We are one; I in them and You in Me, that they may be perfected in unity, so that the world may know that You sent Me, and loved them, even as You have loved Me" (17:22-23).**

Jesus gave great glory to God by spreading the gospel about Heaven, and affirming His words with signs. So when He said, "The glory which You have given Me I have given to them," He was saying that He wants them to also give glory to God by performing signs and wonders.

And Jesus prayed that through the power of the name of

Jesus Christ, His disciples would be able to spread the words that Jesus taught them, cast out demons, cure diseases, and show the power of God. In actuality, the disciples who later received the Holy Spirit performed many great miracles and gave glory to God (Acts 5:15-16). So many signs and wonders occurred through them as recorded in Acts 2:43, *"Everyone kept feeling a sense of awe; and many wonders and signs were taking place through the apostles."*

Jesus wants not only the disciples, but everyone who receives Jesus, to show these powerful works of God. He wants them to be able to cast out demons, speak in new tongues, pick up serpents, not be hurt even if they drink deadly poison, and cure the sick when they lay their hands on them (Mark 16:17-18).

Our church is also giving glory to God through many powerful works of God. When we believed in God's power as recorded in the Bible, and we prayed, the blind opened their eyes, the mute spoke, people in wheelchairs got up and walked, and many people experienced being healed of diseases. Nerves, body tissues, and cells that were once destroyed by burns regenerated, and a person who had stopped breathing and whose body had already become stiffened, came back to life!

In order to perform these kinds of works of God, one must have complete faith. If we have complete faith, and the Lord is in us, and we are in the Lord, there is nothing we can't do. Jesus told us the most important reason we need to become one with Him.

A person who is one with Jesus understands the heart and providence of God, who was from the beginning. Jesus wanted all people to become true children of God who can understand the Father's deep heart. To these kinds of people, as it is written in Proverbs 8:17, *"I love those who love me,"* God shows evidence of His love for them.

During Moses' time when all of Egypt was suffering from all kinds of plagues, the land of Goshen, where God's people lived, did not experience any harm. In the same way, those who are one with the Lord are protected from the enemy devil and Satan, and they receive the blessing of being well and successful in all areas of their lives. God wants to experience this joy from many of His children as they become one with the Lord.

Jesus Wants to Share His Glory in Heaven

"Father, I desire that they also, whom You have given Me, be with Me where I am, so that they may see My glory which You have given Me, for You loved Me before the foundation of the world. O righteous Father, although the world has not known You, yet I have known You; and these have known that You sent Me" (17:24-25).

When we love God and we serve Him, not only will He bless our lives abundantly, but He will also give us unimaginable glory in Heaven. Knowing this very well, Jesus prayed, "I desire that they also, whom You have given Me, be with Me where I am." Jesus wanted to share the eternal glory in Heaven with His beloved disciples, and with all those who received salvation by hearing the gospel that the disciples spread.

Even though they were not at the level of full faith yet, He was just happy with the fact that they acknowledged in their hearts that Jesus was God's Son, and the Savior. During His public ministry, Jesus showed many evidences to help people believe that He came from Heaven. Through the powerful works that Jesus performed and the messages of truth that Jesus preached, people with good hearts believed that Jesus was God's Son, and that He was the Messiah who would save them. As Jesus said, "although the world has not known You," the enemy devil and Satan try to distract the people so they do not believe in God, but these good people stayed alert and fought the good fight and had victory (1 Peter 5:8-9).

"And I have made Your name known to them, and will make it known, so that the love with which You loved Me may be in them, and I in them" (17:26).

"Your [God's] name" contains God's power and authority, heart and love. Jesus showed everything through powerful words, along with signs and wonders. And through acts of forgiveness and compassion, mercy and love, He taught the people about God, who is love.

So what did Jesus mean when He said, "I have made Your name known to them, and will make it known"? He meant that by taking up the cross, shedding all of His water and blood, dying, and then resurrecting, He would complete God's providence. He is making known the heart of God who loved all mankind so much that unsparingly He sent His one and only Son to die on the cross (Romans 8:32).

Therefore the reason Jesus made 'The Father's name' known

to us was so that "the love with which You [God] loved Me may be in them, and I in them." Jesus wants us to receive the love that He received from God, and He wants to be in us. The fact that Jesus is in us means that God's Word is in us (John 14:21), because 'the Word that became flesh' is Jesus. Only those who live according to God's Word can truly say they love God.

We must remember that because Jesus loved God, He completely adhered to the Law while He was in this world, and He completely obeyed to the point of dying on the cross. As a result, He received an incredible amount of God's love.

What difference do you think there was between the love of God that Jesus experienced before He came into this world, and the love of God He experienced after He completed His mission and ascended back into Heaven? Because Jesus is originally one with God, of course He knew God's love, but the depth and weight of God's love that He felt before and that He felt after completing His calling as the Savior were incomparable.

Abraham too, only after he obeyed God's command to sacrifice Isaac, did he experience and realize God's love more clearly. God was probably very happy to see Abraham's faith that was great enough to unsparingly sacrifice his only son, but how awesome Abraham's own emotions must have been when he was able to show God this faith?

Jesus wants us also to realize and experience this deep, deep love of God. When we have faith and act according to God's words, and when we give Him what is most valuable to us because of our love for Him, we can experience a great love of God that we never experienced before.

Chapter 18

Jesus, Who Suffered

Judas Iscariot,
the One Who Betrayed Jesus

After praying to God just before His death, Jesus moved to Gethsemane with His disciples. Gethsemane is a garden located in the western side of the Mount of Olives, situated across the Kidron Valley. Gethsemane was full of overgrown trees and bushes, and it was a rather serene place, so Jesus and His disciples often sought out this place.

The Garden of Gethsemane is the place where right before His suffering on the cross, Jesus prayed so earnestly that His sweat became like drops of blood. Judas Iscariot also knew this place very well. Jesus knew Judas would betray Him; but nonetheless, in order to fulfill His mission as the Savior, Jesus came back to this place.

Jesus Goes to the Garden of Gethsemane

"When Jesus had spoken these words, He went forth with His disciples over the ravine of the Kidron, where there was a garden, in which He entered with His disciples. Now Judas also, who was betraying Him, knew the place, for Jesus had often met there with His disciples" (18:1-2).

In the Gospels of Matthew, Mark, and Luke, all the events that took place between the time Jesus left for the Garden of Gethsemane, and the time Jesus was captured, are recorded in great detail. After arriving at Gethsemane, Jesus told His disciples, 'While I go pray over there, you stay here.' Then He took Peter, James, and John, and went to pray. Making His way through the wild bushes, and going deep into the woods for some time, He told the three to pray there.

"Remain here and keep watch with Me" (Matthew 26:38).

"Pray that you may not enter into temptation" (Luke 22:40).

Going a little further into the distance of about one leap, Jesus put His face to the ground and began to pray very earnestly. Jesus' life depended upon this prayer. The life of Jesus, whose sinless blood would pay for the salvation of all the souls of this world, was at stake. This prayer was a cry out to God for the strength and ability to completely take on the devastating suffering upon the cross. Jesus prayed so fervently with all His strength and might that the small blood vessels in His body burst, turning His drops of sweat into drops of blood (Luke 22:42-44).

In the serene Garden of Gethsemane, the only sound breaking the silence of the night was the sound of Jesus' earnest prayer. After some time, Jesus, who was praying, came to Peter, James, and John. Their flesh being weak, they couldn't fight their fatigue, and they had fallen fast asleep. Jesus was sad to see their weakness, and woke Peter up.

"So, you men could not keep watch with Me for one hour? Keep watching and praying that you may not enter into temptation" (Matthew 26:40-41).

In a little while, Judas Iscariot, along with the soldiers would be coming to capture Jesus. With such a grave event about to take place before their very eyes, Jesus seriously hoped that His disciples would not fall into temptation. So Jesus went a little ways off and continued to pray once again. The disciples tried very hard to pray, but in the end, they could not fight off their slumber. So Jesus was left alone to pray with such might that His sweat became like drops of blood. After three intervals of prayer, Jesus woke up the disciples and said, *"Get up, let us be going; behold, the one who betrays Me is at hand!"* (Matthew 26:46).

Judas Iscariot Betrays Jesus

"Judas then, having received the Roman cohort and officers from the chief priests and the Pharisees, came there with lanterns and torches and weapons. So Jesus, knowing all the things that were coming upon Him, went forth and said to them, 'Whom do you seek?' They answered Him, 'Jesus the Nazarene.' He said to them, 'I am He.' And Judas also, who was betraying Him, was standing with them. So when He said to them, 'I am He,' they drew back and fell to the ground" (18:3-6).

As soon as Jesus finished speaking, flickers of light began to draw near. As the light grew brighter, the sounds of feet thundered everywhere. Shortly thereafter, men with weapons showed themselves under the burning torchlights. In the center stood a man with a familiar face. It was Judas Iscariot, one of the twelve disciples.

The group of soldiers held swords and clubs, as if they came to capture a vicious criminal. We can see how scared they were to capture Jesus. Judas Iscariot as well, even though he brought along a cohort of armed soldiers, was afraid of Jesus' spiritual authority.

"Whom do you seek?"
"Jesus the Nazarene."

Now Judas Iscariot had plotted with the group of soldiers he brought, saying, *"Whomever I kiss, He is the one; seize Him"* (Matthew 26:48). Because Jesus had already set His heart on submitting to God's will to the point of death, He was bold— even before the heavily armed soldiers carrying weapons. People of truth, like Jesus, who stand in the midst of God's will can be bold even if they are dragged to their deaths.

People like these are afraid of going astray from God's will—they are not afraid of losing their life or facing harm. This is because they firmly believe that the only one with true authority over life and death is God the Father. That is why in Matthew 10:28 it says, *"Do not fear those who kill the body but are unable to kill the soul; but rather fear Him who is able to destroy both soul and body in hell."* Jesus boldly disclosed Himself to the cohort of men, saying, "I am He."

At this time, His spiritual power was so great that those who came to capture Him drew back and fell to the ground. In this situation, Judas Iscariot tried to approach Jesus again to kiss Him. *"Hail, Rabbi!"* (Matthew 26:49) Seeing even the deepest part of his heart, Jesus tried to the final moment, to give Judas Iscariot another chance. *"Judas, are you betraying the Son of Man with a kiss?"* (Luke 22:48)

If he had the slightest bit of conscience, since his innermost heart had been revealed, he wouldn't dare kiss his teacher to sell Him. But because Judas Iscariot was already possessed by Satan, he kissed Him and sold Him over. However, all this came to pass for the fulfillment of the plan of salvation by the cross.

In order to hide the fact that he sold Jesus, Judas Iscariot did not directly say, "That person is Jesus the Nazarene." He naturally put on a show and acted as if he had nothing to do with the group of people who came to capture Jesus. Because he was deceitful, he tried to the bitter end to hide the fact that he was the one who sold Jesus.

Jesus Tries to Protect the Disciples

"Therefore He again asked them, 'Whom do you seek?' And they said, 'Jesus the Nazarene.' Jesus answered, 'I told you that I am He; so if you seek Me, let these go their way,' to fulfill the word which He spoke, 'Of those whom You have given Me I lost not one'" (18:7-9).

Even though Jesus revealed who He was, the group of men did not capture Him. So He asked them again. "Whom do you seek?"

There was a reason why Jesus asked again. He was trying to protect the disciples who were with Him. By making the men say with their lips over and over again, "We are seeking Jesus the Nazarene," Jesus was trying to hinder them from putting their hands on anyone else.

They answered, "Jesus the Nazarene." "If you seek Me, let these go their way," said Jesus. In order to make sure the disciples were not harmed in any way, Jesus wisely put a shield of protection around them. Before coming to the Garden of Gethsemane, He had lifted up a prayer of love. In His prayer, He confessed, *"While I was with them, I was keeping them in Your name which You have given Me; and I guarded them and not one of them perished but the son of perdition, so that the Scripture would be fulfilled"* (John 17:12).

Just as He prayed, He worried about the safety of His disciples more than His own, and no matter what dangers He Himself faced, He did not back away. Most of the time, when people feel like they will be disadvantaged, or experience bad consequences, they either shift the responsibility over to someone else, or they will try to flee from the situation. But Jesus readily took on the dangers and hardships by Himself.

> **"Simon Peter then, having a sword, drew it and struck the high priest's slave, and cut off his right ear; and the slave's name was Malchus. So Jesus said to Peter, 'Put the sword into the sheath; the cup which the Father has given Me, shall I not drink it?'"** (18:10-11)

In Peter's eyes, as a disciple under Jesus' care, the situation was very serious. Although Jesus told him that He would be captured in accordance with God's will, even up to this point, Peter did not realize this. Surrounded by a group of men armed with swords and clubs, the situation was dire, for he had no idea what could happen next. At a moment's notice, Peter took out a sword and cut one person's ear off. No one had the time to block, or stop him. The person who cried out in pain and fell to the ground was 'Malchus', a slave of the high priest.

Peter could not just stand by and watch his beloved teacher become captured. Jesus knew Peter's heart, but He gave him a spiritual reprimand, "Put the sword into the sheath; the cup which the Father has given Me, shall I not drink it?" The plan of salvation by the cross was God's providence dating back to the beginning of time. Even if Peter strikes Malchus' ear and tries to prevent the imminent danger at hand, he cannot change the plan of salvation for mankind through Jesus. Seeing Peter striking with the sword, without truly knowing Jesus' heart that wished to obey God's will, rather filled Jesus with sadness.

Jesus Arrested

"So the Roman cohort and the commander and the officers of the Jews, arrested Jesus and bound Him, and led Him to Annas first; for he was father-in-law of Caiaphas, who was high priest that year. Now Caiaphas was the one who had advised the Jews that it was expedient for one man to die on behalf of the people" (18:12-14).

No matter how powerful the Roman cohort, the commander, and the officers of the Jews were, they wouldn't have been able to lay a finger on Jesus if it wasn't for God's will. No one could dare come before His spiritual power. But because it was time, and God permitted it, they bound Jesus and led Him to Annas.

At this time, Caiaphas was the high priest. But why did the people take Jesus to Annas first? This was one of the results of Israel being under the control of Rome. Annas was originally

:: The way to the location where Caiaphas interrogated Jesus

:: Location where Caiaphas interrogated Jesus

the high priest, but under the Roman verdict, Caiaphas was randomly chosen to be the high priest. However, the person the Jews followed and truly acknowledged as the high priest was Annas. Because Annas was Caiaphas' father-in-law, the two had to be in a conspiring relationship. Due to this historical background, although there should only be one high priest, the Four Gospels refer to the high priest as 'high priests', in the plural form (John 7:32, 11:47).

Caiaphas, the high priest, said, *"Nor do you take into account that it is expedient for you that one man die for the people, and that the whole nation not perish"* (John 11:50). Here, he was referring to the death of Jesus. At the time, Caiaphas probably didn't know exactly what he was talking about, but it was as if he was declaring that the death of Jesus was a part of God's provident plan.

The high priests, Annas and Caiaphas were used as evil instruments to carry out the capture and death of Jesus. Because these two men had been piling up great sin upon themselves up to this point, they easily took part in sending Jesus to the cross for crucifixion.

Jesus Stands before
the High Priests

The high priest was the one person who could enter into the holy Temple once a year to offer up sin and guilt offerings to God. At this time, the high priest was chairman of the 'Sanhedrin', the highest ruling council of Israel, so the high priest was a man of great power. For this reason, Jesus was captured and taken before them to be interrogated. As soon as Jesus was captured, the disciples were overcome by shock, fear, and confusion. And sensing the imminent dangers, they all scattered (Mark 14:27; John 16:32). But among them, there were those who followed Jesus all the way to the place of interrogation—of course from a distance, obscuring themselves from the people's eyes.

"Simon Peter was following Jesus, and so was another

disciple. Now that disciple was known to the high priest, and entered with Jesus into the court of the high priest, but Peter was standing at the door outside. So the other disciple, who was known to the high priest, went out and spoke to the doorkeeper, and brought Peter in" (18:15-16).

Peter, who had cut off the ear of Malchus, the high priest's slave, carefully trailed after Jesus. The image of Jesus bound like a serious criminal appeared rather odd and strange to Peter. At that time, there was one other disciple who was also following after Jesus. It was John, who, along with Peter and James, was always at Jesus' side. Peter was able to follow Jesus all the way to Annas' house, but here a problem began. John, who was familiar to the high priest could enter the house, but Peter had to linger around outside the door. But John talked to the doorkeeper so that Peter could also enter into the house.

> "Then the slave-girl who kept the door said to Peter, 'You are not also one of this man's disciples, are you?' He said, 'I am not.' Now the slaves and the officers were standing there, having made a charcoal fire, for it was cold and they were warming themselves; and Peter was also with them, standing and warming himself" (18:17-18).

A slave girl saw Peter and wondered. "You are not also one of this man's disciples, are you?" Suddenly, Peter's mind became cloudy. "I am not."

He could have just remained silent and not denied like this, but the fleshly thought that he might be harmed caused Peter to lie. He had once confessed, *"You are the Christ, the Son of the living God"* (Matthew 16:16). But now that he was frightened and scared, he denied being a disciple of Jesus. Furthermore, as if he had nothing to do with Jesus, he hid among the slaves who were warming themselves by the fire.

Jesus is Interrogated by Annas the High Priest

"The high priest then questioned Jesus about His disciples, and about His teaching. Jesus answered him, 'I have spoken openly to the world; I always taught in synagogues and in the temple, where all the Jews come together; and I spoke nothing in secret. Why do you question Me? Question those who have heard what I spoke to them; they know what I said'" (18:19-21).

Standing before Annas, the most powerful man among the Jews at the time, Jesus was bold. Even though He was in a situation where He could lose His life, He did not try to escape or evade the circumstances. Because He had complete faith in God, He accepted God's providence without any reservation. Also, because He was holy and without sin, He had nothing to fear (Hebrews 7:26).

Annas questioned Jesus about all the things that Jesus taught, and about His disciples, but Jesus mentioned nothing about His disciples. And by saying, "I have spoken openly," and

"I spoke," and "I said," Jesus tried to keep the focus on Himself. He protected His disciples by not once mentioning them to the bitter end.

Jesus came into this world in accordance with God's will. And when He taught the gospel about Heaven, He did so very openly. He taught in the synagogues and the Temple where many Jews gathered. He did not teach secretly in obscure places. The Sadducees and the high priests hired people to spy on Him, so they knew about His teaching. Knowing this fact, Jesus instead asked Annas, "Why do you question Me? Question those who have heard what I spoke to them; they know what I said." The high priest was taken aback. Not only did he have no more reason to question or refute Jesus, but now he was in the situation of being questioned.

> "When He had said this, one of the officers standing nearby struck Jesus, saying, 'Is that the way You answer the high priest?' Jesus answered him, 'If I have spoken wrongly, testify of the wrong; but if rightly, why do you strike Me?' So Annas sent Him bound to Caiaphas the high priest" (18:22-24).

When it seemed as though the situation was turning unfavorably for the high priest, one of the officers watching struck Jesus with his hand. "Is that the way You answer the high priest?" Since He had been arrested, it was expected that He bow down His head with a lowly attitude. But Jesus was not like that at all. He didn't show signs of stooping to the high priest whom they all served. However, there was another reason the officer struck Jesus. He did this because what proceeded made everyone feel Jesus' innocence; so he was trying to break that mood. Of course Jesus knew what was in his heart.

"If I have spoken wrongly, testify of the wrong; but if rightly, why do you strike Me?"

When Jesus spoke of His innocence, the officer tried to cut off what Jesus was saying, but there was nothing more he could say. Annas, feeling that he could do no more with the power that he had, did nothing more to disprove Jesus' innocence, and sent him on to Caiaphas. He could find no charge against Him, but just as they had conferred before, the high priests were trying to drive Jesus to His death anyway. Like this, the high priests knew that Jesus had no sin, and yet they diligently took on the task of being slaves to Satan.

Peter, the One Who Denied Jesus Three Times

"Now Simon Peter was standing and warming himself. So they said to him, 'You are not also one of His disciples, are you?' He denied it, and said, 'I am not.' One of the slaves of the high priest, being a relative of the one whose ear Peter cut off, said, 'Did I not see you in the garden with Him?' Peter then denied it again, and immediately a rooster crowed" (18:25-27).

While Jesus was being interrogated, Peter was just outside in the yard, warming himself with the servants. After strongly denying the slave girl's suspicion, Peter acted as if he had nothing to do with Jesus. However, he could not cast out the fear that someone might recognize him.

Although they had started the fire, because it was deep into the night, and it was nearing dawn, the atmosphere was dark, and lingering fire light made it hard to discern who was who. But the slaves could not help but turn their attention to the stranger who was warming himself among them. They began whispering to each other, "Isn't he a disciple of Jesus? It is he, is he not?" And then, after carefully studying Peter's face, one of them asked, "You are not also one of His disciples, are you?"

Peter replied in haste. "I am not." He had just denied Jesus two times. And just as Peter's level of anxiety from fear began to rise, ultimately, a relative of Malchus, whose ear Peter cut off, recognized him.

"Did I not see you in the garden with Him?" Taken aback, Peter strongly denied. If Peter was bold in the midst of the truth, he would not have denied knowing Jesus. He would have boldly trusted God through all the events that were happening according to His providence. However, Peter was becoming filled with worries like, 'What if they recognize me and capture me?', 'What dangers will I have to face if I am captured?', and 'What will happen next?'

Because he incorporated his fleshly thoughts and denied Jesus once, he ended up denying Him yet again. He didn't just simply deny with, "No". When people didn't seem to believe him, his denial became stronger each time. In Matthew 26:74 it says, *"Then he began to curse and swear, 'I do not know the man!'"* Only after hearing the rooster crow, did Peter jump to his senses.

He then remembered Jesus saying, *"A rooster will not crow until you deny Me three times"* (John 13:38). After running out of Annas' house, Peter wept bitterly. This event of denying Jesus because of his fear remained with Peter for the rest of his life. He regretted for years to come, and his feeling of remorse, embarrassment, and shame could not be erased up until his last days. This is why when he was being martyred, he said, "I am not worthy of hanging on the cross upright as the Lord did," and so he was hung upside down on the cross. Even up to his last moment before death, he simply could not cast this event from his heart.

This event totally changed Peter's life forever. Before, he used to love being in the center of attention, and he was prone to become proud and haughty. Also, he still had some evil that he could not cast out of his heart yet, and his actions were not completely wholesome. But through this trial, his fleshly thoughts came crumbling down, and his heart became humble and lowly. As a result, this incident became a blessed opportunity for Peter to break the frameworks of his mind and circumcise his heart in order to become one of the foremost of Christ's disciples.

God, who looks at the center of a man's heart, knew that through this experience, Peter would rise to become Jesus' top disciple, powerfully fulfilling his calling with his whole life. Even though at the time, Peter experienced great pain in his heart for what he did, this incident became a turning point for Peter to totally transform himself. Seeing the end result of this incident helps us feel God's love as He always works for the good of those who love Him.

What we need to understand here is how ignorant and pitiful we become when we incorporate our fleshly thoughts into our actions. If we incorporate our fleshly thoughts just once, we become easily engulfed in it, and fall even more deeply into it. The deeper we fall into it, the less peace we have in our hearts, and the more anxiety and fear begin developing and encroaching upon our hearts instead. And in order to avoid facing the fear, we may instantaneously lie or act deceitfully. However, if we always have thoughts of the Spirit, even if we may walk through the valley of the shadow of death, our soul can be at peace.

Jesus Stands before Pilate

Standing before Caiaphas the high priest, Jesus is interrogated once more. Matthew chapter 26 depicts this event in detail. The Jews did all they could to find a reason to kill Jesus. They even bought people to be false witnesses, but it was difficult to find evidence to accuse Him. At this time, they remembered something Jesus had said before: *"Destroy this temple, and in three days I will raise it up"* (John 2:19). These words are indicative of Jesus' death and resurrection. However, in their ignorance, the accusers took these words literally, and made an argument for accusation out of it. And in order to gain the evidence that could ultimately lead the case to Jesus' death, they intentionally threw out a leading question to Jesus. *"Tell us whether You are the Christ, the Son of God"* (Matthew 26:63).

Jesus could notice the intention of their questioning, but

He answered plainly. *"You have said it yourself"* (Matthew 26:64). Ultimately, the decision was made that Jesus receive the death sentence for blaspheming against God and His temple. However, because the Jews were under the control of the Rome, they did not have the authority to carry out the death sentence. So they led Him to the Praetorium, in order to turn Him over to Pilate, a prefect of Rome.

"What Accusation Do You Bring Against This Man?"

"Then they led Jesus from Caiaphas into the Praetorium, and it was early; and they themselves did not enter into the Praetorium so that they would not be defiled, but might eat the Passover. Therefore Pilate went out to them and said, 'What accusation do you bring against this Man?' They answered and said to him, 'If this Man were not an evildoer, we would not have delivered Him to you'" (18:28-30).

The "Praetorium" was the palace where a viceroy of Rome lived, and at the time, the viceroy was Pontius Pilate. The Jews led Jesus to the entrance to the Praetorium, but they themselves did not go inside. They considered the uncircumcised Gentiles as unclean, and refrained from coming in contact with them. They were especially more careful not to defile themselves during the Passover, so they tried harder to keep away from Gentiles during this time. They didn't even enter the Praetorium of a Gentile in order that they might not violate the

Law by any chance.

Of course the Gentiles were not excluded from keeping the Passover. Among the Gentiles, if there were some who wanted to participate in the Passover, they could do so after becoming circumcised (Exodus 12:48). On the contrary, even if a person was a Jew, if he had not been circumcised, he could not participate in the Passover. It is not important whether one is a Jew or a Gentile—it is more important whether one is uncircumcised, or circumcised according to God's command.

Like this, traditions of the past teach us that God considers what is in the inside more important than what is on the outside. Even today, it's not important whether we are a Christian on the outside or not. It is more important that we rid ourselves of sin and circumcise our hearts. Now the Jews in Jesus' time professed to abide by the Law; and yet they did not recognize God's Son, and tried to kill Him. This shows how their faith was very superficial and formality-based.

If they had abided strictly by the Law out of their true love for God, then they would not have so harshly persecuted His Son, the One who came into this world in the flesh, and who is originally one with God. On the surface, they claimed to abide by the Law of Moses and even created the tradition of the elders and abided by it, but in the inside, their hearts were evil, and their spiritual eyes were completely covered. Not only did they not recognize the Messiah that they had been waiting for so long; but they tried to kill Him through the cruelest punishment available—the crucifixion.

As if he knew the customs of the Jews who did not enter the Praetorium to keep the Passover, Pilate came out to them and asked: "What accusation do you bring against this Man?" "If this Man were not an evildoer, we would not have delivered Him to you."

In a legitimate trial, the accuser needs to tell the judge every detail of their accusation. Then, in order to decipher the truth, the judge needs to give the accused person a fair chance to defend himself. However, without even making a clear accusation, the high priests and the elders obstinately accused Jesus of being an evildoer. In reality, they themselves knew Jesus had no sin. But when their people began following Jesus, and their vested authority seemed to be at stake, they became determined to accuse Jesus as an evildoer.

However, the accusations the Jews made, about blaspheming the Temple and God was not considered a sin according to Roman law. Moreover, even with one glance, one could see that this was clearly a conspiracy conjured up out of jealousy by the crowd of people associated with the high priest. To Pilate's eyes, it was more amazing to see Jesus not saying a single word of protest to the people who were making slanderous accusations against Him (Mark 15:5).

So when Pilate finally declared, *"I find no guilt in this man"* (Luke 23:4), the high priest and the crowd responded with a violent uproar.

"Take Him Yourselves, and Judge Him According to Your Law"

"So Pilate said to them, 'Take Him yourselves, and

judge Him according to your law.' The Jews said to him, 'We are not permitted to put anyone to death,' to fulfill the word of Jesus which He spoke, signifying by what kind of death He was about to die" (18:31-32).

Pilate did not want to get involved in the Jews' religious problems. He wanted to quickly disengage himself from this cumbersome case. Then he heard that Jesus was from Galilee (Luke 23:5-6). In Israel at the time, the region of Judea, which was centered around Jerusalem, was under the authority of Pilate, but the northern region of Galilee was under the jurisdiction of Herod (Herod Antipas).

Ever so timely, Herod was in Jerusalem at this time because of the Passover, so Pilate sent Jesus to him right away (Luke 23:6-7). Herod was glad. He had heard about Jesus for a long time, and he wanted to witness with his own eyes, the miracles that Jesus performed. But all his expectations came crumbling down. When he couldn't even get an answer to any of his questions, let alone a miracle, he and his soldiers mocked Jesus. Then, after putting on a gorgeous robe on Him, he sent Him back to Pilate (Luke 23:8-11).

Pilate still wanted to turn the judgment over to the Jews. "Take Him yourselves, and judge Him according to your law." But the kind of punishment the Jews were looking for was not the kind that ends with simple pain. They wanted Jesus to be crucified.

Jesus already knew what kind of death He would face. That is why He said in John 12:32, *"And I, if I am lifted up from the earth, will draw all men to Myself."* Just as this verse foretold, the high priest and the crowd shouted for the execution on the cross, and pressured Pilate so this would happen. They played the role of making Jesus' words come true.

"Are You the King of the Jews?"

> "Therefore Pilate entered again into the Praetorium, and summoned Jesus and said to Him, 'Are You the King of the Jews?' Jesus answered, 'Are you saying this on your own initiative, or did others tell you about Me?'" (18:33-34)

Pilate felt humiliated in front of the crowd that vehemently called out for the death of Jesus. Although their accusations seemed to be mere speculations, because such a large crowd was intensely requesting for the execution by the cross, he felt quite helpless. The crowd had now turned into a mob, and it seemed as though their shouting was beginning to shake the foundations of the Praetorium. Not knowing what to do, Pilate came back inside the Praetorium and questioned Jesus. "Are You the King of the Jews?"

Jesus was so peaceful that one could not believe that He was standing in the face of His death sentence. At Pilate's question, Jesus answered with another question. "Are you saying this on your own initiative, or did others tell you about Me?"

By physical lineage, Jesus was born as the descendent of the most excellent King David. Of course He was conceived by the Holy Spirit through the Virgin Mary, and Mary's husband,

Joseph, was a descendant of David (Isaiah 11:10). Also, when Jesus was born, the three magi from the east said, *"Where is He who has been born King of the Jews? For we saw His star in the east and have come to worship Him"* (Matthew 2:2). So not only is Jesus King of the Jews; but spiritually, He is also the King of kings (Revelations 17:14).

Jesus' answer was a wise response that showed how meaningless and insignificant Pilate's question was. Pilate knew what Jesus taught and what kind of work He did, because he had heard about it all along. And meeting Jesus firsthand, he felt the spiritual majesty that one could not feel from any other king of this world. So when Jesus asked whether he was asking this question because he truly wanted to know if He really was the king of the Jews, or whether he was asking simply because of the Jews' accusation, Pilate was both shocked and embarrassed.

> **"Pilate answered, 'I am not a Jew, am I? Your own nation and the chief priests delivered You to me; what have You done?' Jesus answered, 'My kingdom is not of this world. If My kingdom were of this world, then My servants would be fighting so that I would not be handed over to the Jews; but as it is, My kingdom is not of this realm'" (18:35-36).**

Pilate gave Jesus a chance to defend Himself so He could prove His own innocence. "I am not a Jew, am I? Your own nation and the chief priests delivered You to me; what have You done?" But the reply he received was one he did not expect. "My kingdom is not of this world. If My kingdom were of this world, then My servants would be fighting so that I would not be handed over to the Jews; but as it is, My kingdom is not of this realm."

Pilate considered the Jews and Jesus as of the same nation. However, Jesus clearly distinguished Himself from the Jews. It all depended on whether one perceived with spiritual eyes, or eyes of the flesh. If you think deep in the spirit about Jesus' words, you can figure out the origin of Jesus. By origin, Jesus is one with God, and as His Son, He has unlimited authority and power. But in order to fulfill the providence of salvation, He came into this world. If He had come into this world to become its king, as the people of this world thought He would, armies of angels would watch over Him and protect Him. However, Jesus' purpose for coming into this world was to become the atoning sacrifice for mankind that became slaves to sin. The result of all this would ultimately make Him the King of kings and Lord of lords.

"I Find No Guilt in Him"

"Therefore Pilate said to Him, 'So You are a king?' Jesus answered, 'You say correctly that I am a king. For this I have been born, and for this I have come into the world, to testify to the truth. Everyone who is of the truth hears My voice.' Pilate said to Him, 'What is truth?' And when he had said this, he went out again to the Jews and said to them, 'I find no guilt in Him'" (18:37-38).

Jesus spoke with spiritual meaning, but Pilate could not understand. As if he didn't even know what he was asking himself, he asked again: "So You are a king?" "You say *correctly* that I am a king. For this I have been born, and for this I have come into the world, to testify to the truth. Everyone who is of the truth hears My voice."

A person who has a good heart, and who fears God from the center of his heart knows and believes that Jesus is God's Son, and that He came into this world as the Savior. But because Pilate could not understand Jesus' spiritual words, he became frustrated. Any more interrogation would be meaningless. For the last time, he threw out this question: "What is truth?"

He wasn't expecting an answer. This question was just an attempt to clear up his confused heart. Right away, he went outside to the crowd. As soon as they saw Pilate, the crowd began to stir again. At this time, Pilate shouted out at them. No matter how much a crowd wanted to hear it, he could not sentence an innocent man as sinner. "I find no guilt in Him."

Jesus, who was being interrogated in Pilate's court, was very calm and at peace. He did not object to any words, or show anger. One could not find any evil in Him. Only with superior wisdom and spiritual significance did He answer the questions given to Him. If He had any hint of evil in Him, He would have protested with harsh words or burst out in anger and frustration in order to appeal for His innocence. However, Jesus had no evil, so He answered every question with peace, and in the spirit.

But it is not that Jesus spoke with spiritual words because He could not clearly justify Himself as sinless. He had already humbly accepted in His heart to bear the suffering on the cross to submit to God's will to the point of death. Here again we can see that Jesus' suffering on the cross is God's will and providence.

> "'But you have a custom that I release someone for you at the Passover; do you wish then that I release for you the King of the Jews?' So they cried out again, saying, 'Not this Man, but Barabbas.' Now Barabbas was a robber" (18:39-40).

In order to release Jesus, Pilate thought up a ruse. To win the Jews' hearts, every year at Passover, the viceroy released one prisoner whom the people chose.

Pilate thought Jesus' capture was a simple conspiracy of the high priests and elders, but the crowd's reaction was a surprise to him. The high priests' and elders' influence over the people was already too great. "Not this Man, but Barabbas."

Barabbas was a notorious criminal who was imprisoned for murder and causing an uproar. But the Jews wanted to hang Jesus, who was sinless, in place of Barabbas. The Jews became a faithful tool for Satan who wanted to kill Jesus.

In order to kill Jesus, Satan moved their evil hearts; however, hidden behind all this was God's providence. Satan thought that if he nailed Jesus on the cross and killed Him, his own power and authority over this world would be eternal. However, he was actually digging his own grave when he thought this. He did not realize that the law of death did not apply to Jesus, because Jesus was sinless.

What do you think was going through Jesus' mind in the midst of the people's angry threats and demands that were tossing and turning like a raging sea? Of course Jesus knew He would be interrogated, and condemned to take up the cross because of God's providence and hidden will; but Jesus too, was at the crossroads of emotions at this time.

How do you think Jesus felt, as He saw the very same people who had welcomed Him with palm leaves a couple days ago, now shouting for His crucifixion? He wasn't sad or frustrated because He was being forced to suffer without proper cause. No. He wasn't even scared or filled with fear for what He was about to face. He was, however, devastated by the fact that the very people who were created in the image of God were sinning and obeying the voice of Satan and acting as his slaves.

On the other hand, Jesus also looked back at the ministry He had led thus far. He lifted up a sacrifice of thanksgiving to God, because from the moment He came down to this world up to this point, all the events that had passed occurred according to God's will. Joy and thanksgiving filled Jesus' heart, because through His suffering, God's will and providence would finally be fulfilled and completed.

Chapter 19

Jesus on the Cross

Pilate Authorizes
the Death Sentence

Pilate was in a serious dilemma. Because Jesus had no sin, Pilate was going to release Him according to the customs of the Passover, but the Jews opposed this so strongly that he did not know what to do. The crowd of Jews gathered in front of the Praetorium was shouting for him to release the murderer, Barabbas, and instead kill Jesus, who was without sin. At this point, the crowd had already turned into a mob. *"Have nothing to do with that righteous Man; for last night I suffered greatly in a dream because of Him"* (Matthew 27:19). Just then Pilate remembered the message his wife sent him. However, in the midst of the clamor and chaos that would not die down, he had to make a decision.

The Reason Jesus Was Flogged and Crowned with the Crown of Thorns

"Pilate then took Jesus and scourged Him. And the soldiers twisted together a crown of thorns and put it on His head, and put a purple robe on Him; and they began to come up to Him and say, 'Hail, King of the Jews!' and to give Him slaps in the face" (19:1-3).

Pilate was going to have Jesus flogged, and when the crowd died down a little, he was going to release Him (Luke 23:22). At the time, Roman soldiers were strong and well-trained. The whips that they used were leather straps tied with sharp bones or imbedded pieces of metal, so just looking at the straps made people cringe.

Without even a bit of compassion, the soldiers began beating down on Jesus with the straps. Each time the straps hit and clung onto Jesus' body, bits of His flesh came off and parts of His bones were exposed. From each wound made by the straps spewed out streams of red blood. After that, the soldiers took a long branch with sharp thorns and crudely twisted it into a crown, put it on Jesus' head and pressed down on it with all their might. The sharp thorns pierced into the skin and spurted out blood. Then they placed a purple robe on Him, ridiculed Him, and slapped Him in the face. Purple linen and crown symbolize kingship, but they clothed Jesus with the purple robe and crown in order to mock Him. Some soldiers even bowed as if they were being courteous to a king and contemptuously said, "Hail, King of the Jews!"

Yes, Pilate commanded for this to take place, but it did not occur according to his will. As it is written in Isaiah 53:5, *"But He was pierced through for our transgressions, He was crushed for our iniquities; the chastening for our well-being fell upon Him, and by His scourging we are healed,"* this event was already prophesied.

It is also written in 1 Peter 2:24, *"For by His wounds you were healed."* Therefore we can see all these events occurred as part of the fulfillment of God's providence. And as it says, *"Without shedding of blood there is no forgiveness"* (Hebrews 9:22), Jesus was scourged and He shed His blood in order to pay for our sins. So through this sacrifice, sin, which is the root of all sicknesses and problems, was atoned for.

And the reason Jesus had to wear the crown of thorns was part of God's providence to atone for all the sins we commit in thoughts. People usually have thoughts of untruth, which is contrary to God's will. The enemy Satan controls these thoughts so that people grow distant from God and are unable to have faith. If man continues to receive the thoughts of untruth that the enemy Satan keeps giving to him, the end result is eternal death, or Hell. This is why Jesus received the crown of thorns and paid for all the sins of our thoughts.

Even while suffering from the pain of the piercing straps and crown of thorns, Jesus did not resist. He quietly took the suffering (Isaiah 53:7). Rather, He felt sorrow for the people who were mocking and flogging Him. He felt pity for them, because they were partaking in these evil acts out of ignorance. But knowing that this was the way to bringing peace between mankind and God and the way to salvation for the world that was going to the way of death, Jesus had patience and persevered (2 Corinthians 5:18-20).

> "Pilate came out again and said to them, 'Behold, I am bringing Him out to you so that you may know that I find no guilt in Him.' Jesus then came out, wearing the crown of thorns and the purple robe. Pilate said to them, 'Behold, the Man!'" (19:4-5).

In order to calm the crowd and to establish a cause to release Jesus, Pilate had Jesus flogged, and then brought Him out of the Praetorium. "Behold, I am bringing Him out to you so that you may know that I find no guilt in Him."

Stained with blood from being pierced by the straps and the crown of thorns, Jesus' face was beyond recognition. Even while seeing Jesus, who was sinless, standing before them in such a pitiful state, the crowd didn't even feel a hint of guilt in their conscience. Seeing the blood actually made them even more ruthless. Pilate's last strategy to release Jesus came crumbling down.

> "So when the chief priests and the officers saw Him, they cried out saying, 'Crucify, crucify!' Pilate said to them, 'Take Him yourselves and crucify Him, for I find no guilt in Him.' The Jews answered him, 'We have a law, and by that law He ought to die because He made Himself out to be the Son of God'" (19:6-7).

In the midst of the crowd, the high priests and officers

shouted for Jesus to be crucified. The crowd was heavily agitated by their arousal, so drawing out the verdict of execution by crucifixion was just a matter of time. In reality, they too, saw the power Jesus performed. They knew He healed the sick and showed mercy and compassion to the poor and the weak. But they were listening to the voice of Satan as they shouted for Jesus' crucifixion and moved the crowd to do the same.

The fear that Pilate felt at this time is clearly recorded in the document he sent to the Emperor Caesar in Rome. This document, which is now preserved in the Mosque of St. Sofia, in Turkey, records information about how Jesus was arrested, interrogated, and executed.

"I then ordered him to be scourged, hoping this would satisfy them, but it only increased their fury. I then called for a basin and washed my hands in the presence of the clamorous multitude, thus testifying that in my judgment Jesus of Nazareth had done nothing worthy of death; but in vain; it was his life these wretches thirsted for.

Often in our civil commotions have I witnessed the furious animosities of the multitude, but nothing can be compared to what I witnessed on this occasion. It might have been truly said that on this occasion all the phantoms of the infernal regions had assembled at Jerusalem. The crowd appeared not to walk, but to be borne off and whiled as a vortex, rolling along in living waves from the portals of the Praetorium, even unto Mt. Zion, with howling, screams, shrieks and vociferations, such as were never heard in the sedition of Pannonia, or in the tumults of the forum."

Pilate was suddenly filled with fear that there might be an uprising, and that he might lose his own life. After deciding there is nothing more he could do, he tried to clear responsibility of this judgment by turning Jesus over to the people so they can handle the situation on their own. "Take Him yourselves and crucify Him, for I find no guilt in Him."

As judge, Pilate clearly knew Jesus had no sin. However, he was not able to make a fair judgment call, and turned complete responsibility over to the people. Fearing the people, he gave into their demand and turned an innocent man over to them. How cowardly his decision was!

God does not just randomly give one person an evil role, and another person a good role. He works with every person according to the center of each person's heart. In the fulfillment of the plan of salvation by Jesus' sacrifice on the cross, each person involved was used according to the kind of vessel he or she was.

"We have a law, and by that law He ought to die because He made Himself out to be the Son of God."

When they said 'law' here, they were referring to "the Law of Moses" that they strictly adhered to. The Jews were arguing that because Jesus called Himself God's Son, He had committed a sin that is punishable by death. The Scripture that supports this is found in Exodus 20:7, *"You shall not take the name of the LORD your God in vain, for the LORD will not leave him unpunished who takes His name in vain."* Also, Leviticus

24:16 says, *"Moreover, the one who blasphemes the name of the LORD shall surely be put to death; all the congregation shall certainly stone him. The alien as well as the native, when he blasphemes the Name, shall be put to death."*

The Jews thought that Jesus was a person just like them. That is why when He called Himself the Son of God, they thought He was blaspheming God's name. However, Jesus never took God's name in vain, or blasphemed His name. He only gave glory to God. It was because of their ignorance and evil that they did not recognize Jesus, who was indeed the true Son of God.

If they had correctly known God's heart and will that is contained in the Law, they would not have tried to kill Jesus, who came as the Messiah. But because of their perception of 'righteousness' of the Law based on their own thoughts and frameworks, they could not make a truly right decision. They rather thought killing Jesus was the 'right' thing to do.

"He Who Delivered Me to You Has the Greater Sin"

"Therefore when Pilate heard this statement, he was even more afraid; and he entered into the Praetorium again and said to Jesus, 'Where are You from?' But Jesus gave him no answer. So Pilate said to Him, 'You do not speak to me? Do You not know that I have authority to release You, and I have authority to crucify You?' Jesus answered, 'You would have no authority over Me, unless it had been given you from above; for this reason he who delivered Me to you has the greater sin'" (19:8-11).

The Jews declared that they needed to kill Jesus because He claimed to be "God's Son". On the one hand, Pilate, after hearing this statement, became even more afraid. Even though Pilate was a Gentile, He felt an unexplainable fear in front of Jesus, because He was different from any other person, and He had spiritual power like none other. Not knowing what to do, Pilate returned to the Praetorium and asked Jesus: "Where are You from?"

Jesus did not answer. He knew that even if He told Pilate, Pilate would still turn Him over to the crowd because he feared them. It is just as it is stated in John 2:24-25, *"But Jesus, on His part, was not entrusting Himself to them, for He knew all men, and because He did not need anyone to testify concerning man, for He Himself knew what was in man."* Pilate himself did not even know his own heart. He just felt frustrated with Jesus, who didn't answer him. So he asked again: "Do You not know that I have authority to release You, and I have authority to crucify You?" Even though he was looking around nervously and feeling anxious due to the pressure from the Jews, Pilate was boasting that he had the power to change the situation. At this, Jesus gave him an answer that Pilate might, or might not comprehend: "You would have no authority over Me, unless it had been given you from above."

Thinking that there was no one else in all Judea who had greater power than he did, Pilate was not able to understand this statement. Because all power and authority belongs to God, even if someone is a viceroy of a powerful nation like Rome, he is under God's authority (Romans 13:1). Therefore if God does not permit it, no one can do anything. Not knowing this truth,

Pilate was strutting his power.

Because God knew Pilate was rather shallow, and would turn Jesus over to the people, He permitted this situation, as a part of His providence. When a person with a shallow heart faces a difficult situation, he will make a decision that will benefit himself. These characteristics do not come to the surface in normal circumstances, but when facing hard or pressing circumstances, a person of this type will either sneak off and out of the situation, or come up with a lie. If a person has evil in his heart, that evil is bound to surface up in one way or another.

Finally, in order to retain his status and power, Pilate gives in to the Jews' demand. However, the greater responsibility falls upon Judas Iscariot, who delivered Jesus to him. That is why Jesus said his sin is greater.

> **"As a result of this Pilate made efforts to release Him, but the Jews cried out saying, 'If you release this Man, you are no friend of Caesar; everyone who makes himself out to be a king opposes Caesar.' Therefore when Pilate heard these words, he brought Jesus out, and sat down on the judgment seat at a place called The Pavement, but in Hebrew, Gabbatha" (19:12-13).**

Pilate, in his own way, tried hard to release Jesus. He was not comfortable executing someone who had committed no crime, and his wife's dream bothered him. Just then the Jews said what pushed Pilate to the edge: "If you release this Man, you are no friend of Caesar; everyone who makes himself out to be a king opposes Caesar." Whether in the East or West, the penalty for treason is death. Especially for a politician, it is a fatal crime, and the lives of even his family members could be at stake. Pushed to the ledge, Pilate knew that he too, would face some kind of aftermath from this event.

The Trial of Pilate Who Feared the Crowd

"Now it was the day of preparation for the Passover; it was about the sixth hour. And he said to the Jews, 'Behold, your King!' So they cried out, 'Away with Him, away with Him, crucify Him!' Pilate said to them, 'Shall I crucify your King?' The chief priests answered, 'We have no king but Caesar.' So he then handed Him over to them to be crucified" (19:14-16).

In a state of grabbing at the last straw, Pilate sat on the judge's seat and asked the Jews one last time: "Shall I crucify your King?" Even though he clearly knew Jesus had committed no crime, Pilate's heart was shaken because he saw himself in a dire situation. His shallow and flighty heart was clearly revealed. The Jews were so determined to see Jesus' death that they lost all sense of reason to the point they didn't even know what they were saying. "We have no king but Caesar."

The Jews said they had no other king but Caesar, the emperor of the Roman Empire, the nation ruling over Israel at that time. This was like people suffering in a colony under the rule of an enemy nation betraying their own nation and swearing allegiance to the enemy nation. They were not hesitating to say things that were contrary to their national beliefs, and they were even selling the name of God, their Father and King. They were so obsessed with killing Jesus that they even put aside their faith in the LORD God. They were totally immersed in their laws and self-righteousness that they acted against God's will, and in order to fulfill their goal, they even put away their faith.

Rather than being accused of being a traitor, Pilate decided that it would be better to side with the Jews. So finally he gave the verdict to kill Jesus. Right before this, he brought out a basin of water and washed his hands before the crowd. He intentionally did this to show that he has nothing to do with this execution. *"I am innocent of this Man's blood; see to that yourselves"* (Matthew 27:24).

Seeing that their demand was being met, the people became even more drastic in their actions. *"His blood shall be on us and on our children!"* (Matthew 27:25) They had no idea what kind of catastrophe these words would later bring upon themselves and their children. The many years the Jews had to spend scattered about after losing their country, and the death of millions of Jews at the hands of the Nazi army during World War II are repercussions that cannot be totally severed from these words.

Jesus' death was a part of God's providence that was planned before the beginning of time. During the fulfillment of this plan, each person was used either as a good tool, or an evil tool, according to the type of vessel he or she was. In Pilate's case, because his heart was flighty and unrighteous, he ended up playing a crucial role in the death of Jesus.

Jesus Is Nailed on the Cross

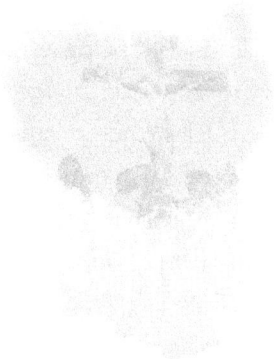

After He was sentenced to execution, Jesus received more severe floggings. Usually, Roman soldiers would take off the convict's clothing, bend them over and tie them to a post or frame and flog them without mercy. Just from this alone, many convicts are said to have fainted or lost their lives. From this severe flogging, Jesus also was in a state of debilitation. Without a hint of caring, the Roman soldiers made Jesus carry the heavy cross.

> "They took Jesus, therefore, and He went out, bearing His own cross, to the place called the Place of a Skull, which is called in Hebrew, Golgotha. There they crucified Him, and with Him two other men, one on either side, and Jesus in between" (19:17-18).

Once a person is sentenced to execution by the cross, he had to carry the cross upon which he would be nailed, all the way to Golgotha, the place where he would ultimately be nailed to that very cross. While taking each heavy step on the narrow way of "Via Dolorosa", Jesus fell many times. Although He was God's Son, because He had flesh and bones like us, He couldn't help but become exhausted. Becoming impatient, the Roman soldiers finally made a person named Simon of Cyrene (today's Libya) carry the cross and follow after Jesus (Luke 23:26).

What do you think went through Jesus' mind as He carried the cross from Pilate's Praetorium all the way to Golgotha? He did not simply think about the heaviness of the cross or the suffering He was feeling with His flesh. As He carried the cross, He recalled many scenes. He thought about God's purpose in creating man, and the significance of cultivating mankind. He also thought about the ultimate reason why He had to be given up as the atoning sacrifice, and deep within His heart He lifted up a prayer of thanksgiving.

As it is written in John chapter 1, Jesus, who was the Word that came to this world in flesh, is originally one with God, and He was with God from the very beginning. Therefore He knew everything from the moment of creation. When God created the heavens and the earth and all the living things in between, the Scripture states, *"And God saw that it was good"* (Genesis 1:25). But when things began to change due to man's sin, Jesus felt the pain, alongside the Father God.

From a human standpoint, with all His followers gone, with no strength or power, Jesus was no more than a poor, miserable criminal. However, from a spiritual standpoint, this was the glorious moment when Jesus would fulfill the greatest mission of love. This was the moment the One who had unlimited glory, authority, and power gave everything up in order to become the atoning sacrifice for the sin of mankind. This was the historic moment when the great mission—God's secret plan from the beginning of time, the salvation of mankind, would be fulfilled.

Finally, they arrived at the hill of Golgotha. Golgotha, which in Hebrew means "the skull", was a site of execution just outside the walls of Jerusalem. In order to maximize the sense of indignity, in front of all the onlookers, the soldiers took off Jesus' clothing and laid Him down on the frame of the cross. Then they nailed His hands and His feet. The echoing sound from the banging hammer brought cold chills into the hearts of the onlookers.

The form of the gigantic cross was raised as if it was shooting up into the sky. As the weight of the whole body shifted to the nailed hands and feet, inexpressible pain shot throughout the whole body. Crucifixion was the cruelest form of execution. Compared to other forms of punishment, the execution by crucifixion made the person being crucified suffer pain for a very long time. Once in a while there may have been cases where the executioners may have shown mercy to the criminal by breaking his shinbones, or piercing his sides so he can experience a quicker death. But in most cases, the criminals were left to suffer a slow death lasting from one to several days. Besides the pain from being nailed to the cross, the crucified person also had to suffer from severe dehydration, and the deterioration of all of his body organs due to poor circulation. On top of that, he even had to deal with the bugs that swarmed around due to the smell of blood!

However, Jesus suffered from 9 in the morning until 3 in the afternoon. Contrary to the norm, He died within 6 hours. At this time, two robbers were crucified along with Jesus—one on each side of Him. This was a secret, devious calculation by the Jews who wanted to make Jesus look like He was paying the price for some sin, just like the two robbers.

> "Pilate also wrote an inscription and put it on the cross. It was written, 'JESUS THE NAZARENE, THE KING OF THE JEWS.' Therefore many of the Jews read this inscription, for the place where Jesus was crucified was near the city; and it was written in Hebrew, Latin and in Greek. So the chief priests of the Jews were saying to Pilate, 'Do not write, "The King of the Jews"; but that He said, "I am King of the Jews."' Pilate answered, 'What I have written I have written'" (19:19-22).

Pilate was a coward that turned Jesus over to the people for fear of them, but in the end, he listened to his conscience. So he made the soldiers write an inscription, "JESUS THE NAZARENE, THE KING OF THE JEWS" and put it on the cross. He did not make this inscription in order to mock Jesus or make fun of Him. Pilate really felt that Jesus was truly the King of the Jews.

The high priests saw the inscription and were outraged. As if they were victims of some grave offense, they did not hesitate to ask Pilate to change the inscription to say, "He said 'I am King of the Jews.'" To the very end, they were trying to justify their behavior by adding the words, "He said" so that Jesus would look like a sinner. But by saying, "What I have written I have written," Pilate expressed once again, that in his opinion, Jesus had committed no crime.

Even in this situation, Jesus was thinking about God's love. He felt the love of God, who did not even spare His one and only Son to save the people who had become slaves to the enemy devil and Satan and were going to the way of death. Concerning God's love, 1 John 4:9-10 reads, *"By this the love of God was manifested in us, that God has sent His only begotten Son into the world so that we might live through Him. In this is love, not that we loved God, but that He loved us and sent His Son to be the propitiation for our sins."*

The Providence behind the Soldiers' Dividing His Outer Garments and Casting for His Inner Clothing

"Then the soldiers, when they had crucified Jesus, took His outer garments and made four parts, a part to every soldier and also the tunic; now the tunic was seamless, woven in one piece. So they said to one another, 'Let us not tear it, but cast lots for it, to decide whose it shall be'; this was to fulfill the Scripture: 'THEY DIVIDED MY OUTER GARMENTS AMONG THEM, AND FOR MY CLOTHING THEY CAST LOTS'" (19:23-24).

After crucifying Jesus, the soldiers did something they usually did not do. While talking amongst themselves, they decided to divide up Jesus' outer and inner clothing and each take a piece of it. They divided the outer garments into four parts, one for each soldier, and then they pondered about what to do with His tunic, since it was of one piece, and finally they decided to cast lots to see who would get it. "Let us not tear it, but cast lots for it, to decide whose it shall be."

On the outside, it simply looked as if these soldiers were dividing up the clothes and casting lots on their own, but from a spiritual perspective, that is not the case. This event was already prophesied in Psalm 22:18, *"They divide my garments among them, and for my clothing they cast lots."* Even though the soldiers probably thought they were just doing what they wanted to do, all these events occurred precisely under God's providence. By all means, Jesus' clothes were not expensive, or valuable enough for the soldiers to want to divide and keep for themselves. But why did they divide His garments and cast lots for His tunic?

If we look at Israel's history after 70 A.D., we can see why this happened. Because Jesus was the King of the Jews, His clothing symbolizes Israel, or the Jewish people. The fact that the soldiers divided Jesus' garments into four and each one took one part foreshadowed the way the nation of Israel's identity would be obliterated by the Gentiles, and the way its people would be scattered all throughout the land. This was a prophecy that the nation of Israel would ultimately be destroyed by the Romans, because the Jews themselves killed Jesus, who came as their King and their Messiah.

In actuality, in 70 A.D., the Roman General Titus captured Israel, and the Temple was totally destroyed so that not one stone was left on top of another. And 1,100,000 Jews were killed, with just about 9,000 or so surviving. And those who survived were either taken captive, or scattered about. This is one of the reasons the Jewish people are still scattered all over the world today.

While Jesus' outer garments symbolize the physical aspect of Israel, His inner clothing symbolizes the Israel people's inner heart. The fact that Jesus' tunic was seamless, or woven in one piece, means that ever since Israel's birth through Jacob, to the current times, its heritage was never mixed with Gentiles, meaning that the nation of Israel is made up of a homogeneous people. And the fact that the tunic was not torn like the outer garments, but was taken in one piece after casting of lots symbolizes the fact that their nationality, or their heart for serving God, is not torn, but well-protected.

This was a prophecy that although the nation was destroyed by the hands of Gentiles, and its territory was obliterated, Israel's heart toward God did not change. Just as Jesus' tunic was woven in one piece and could not be torn, the hearts of the Israelites could not be torn, and their nation was reborn. Nineteen hundred years after losing their sovereignty, on May 14, 1948, the nation of Israel gained its independence and surprised the whole world. And in just a short period of time after that, the nation of Israel developed into one of the most prosperous nations in the world, proving that the Israeli people are a distinguished people.

"But standing by the cross of Jesus were His mother, and His mother's sister, Mary the wife of Clopas, and Mary Magdalene. When Jesus then saw His mother, and the disciple whom He loved standing nearby, He said to His mother, 'Woman, behold, your son!' Then He said to the disciple, 'Behold, your mother!' From that hour the disciple took her into his own household" (19:25-27).

Near Jesus' cross, there were people who wanted to mock Him and watch His death; but also by His cross was His beloved disciple and the women who received His grace. These people were in a situation where they would have died; but because of Jesus, they received new life, and their life of woe transformed into a life of value. The moment they heard that Jesus was captured, they ran to Jesus, and until the moment He drew His last breath, they never left His side. Even while suffering on the cross, Jesus looked after the Virgin Mary, saying to her, "Woman, behold, your son!" and saying to him "Behold, your mother!"

Here, 'son' refers to His beloved disciple, John. Jesus was telling Mary that she should take John as her own son now, and to John He was asking him as a child of God, to serve Mary as he would his own mother.

And the reason why Jesus called Mary 'woman', instead of 'mother', holds a spiritual significance. Jesus was simply born through the body of the Virgin Mary, not through her egg. He was conceived by the Holy Spirit, and is one with God. The Creator God is who He is (Exodus 3:14), and He is the first and the last (Revelations 1:17, 2:8), so He cannot have a mother. That is why Jesus did not call Mary 'mother' here.

Even though she was not Jesus' mother, He knew Mary's heart. Jesus understood Mary, who had watched Jesus grow and mature from birth, and He understood her heart better than anyone else. How could Mary express the pain of watching Jesus, whom she loved more than her own life, dying such a miserable death on the cross?

> **"Lord, my Lord! By God's grace He let You come into this world through this poor and lowly maidservant, but watching You up there from here below, my heart does not know what to do. As I watched You every moment I raised You, I felt as if I was meeting the Father in Heaven... I was always careful, protecting every hair on Your head... as I watched You grow, I always worried in my heart so You would not be harmed, so He would not be dishonored in any way... but now that I must witness this miserable suffering, what do I do, Lord? What do I do? For my poor heart cannot be comforted..."**

Knowing Mary's heart very well, Jesus beseeched John to serve her like his own mother. This teaches us that in faith, everyone is sister and brother, in one family. Matthew 12:48-50 describes that: *"But Jesus answered the one who was telling Him and said, 'Who is My mother and who are My brothers?' And stretching out His hand toward His disciples, He said, 'Behold My mother and My brothers! For whoever does the will of My Father who is in heaven, he is My brother and sister and mother,"* teaching us about the 'spiritual family'.

From this moment on, John served Mary as his own mother, and took her into his house. While listening to Mary talk about the way Jesus grew up, he gained greater assurance that He was truly the Christ; and therefore was able to take on his calling more wholeheartedly.

Jesus Dies on the Cross

"After this, Jesus, knowing that all things had already been accomplished, to fulfill the Scripture, said, 'I am thirsty.' A jar full of sour wine was standing there; so they put a sponge full of the sour wine upon a branch of hyssop and brought it up to His mouth. Therefore when Jesus had received the sour wine, He said, 'It is finished!' And He bowed His head and gave up His spirit" (19:28-30).

Jesus knew He didn't have much longer to live. And the closer He drew near to His death, the more His heart pressed for all the souls. "I am thirsty."

Since He had been shedding blood for a long time under the hot sun, of course He was thirsty. But when Jesus said, "I am thirsty," it wasn't simply because He was feeling physically thirsty. This was also an expression of His heart thirsting for the salvation of all souls dying due to their sin.

The people who did not understand this spiritual meaning

behind what Jesus said, put a sponge full of sour wine on a branch of hyssop and put it to His mouth. The prophecy from Psalm 69:21 that says, *"They also gave me gall for my food and for my thirst they gave me vinegar to drink"* was fulfilled. Spiritually, wine symbolizes blood. Jesus drinking the sour wine symbolizes the fact that He completed the Law of the Old Testament with love, and that He took upon Himself the sins and curses of all mankind. In the Old Testament times, before Jesus came into the world, every time a person sinned, he had to kill an animal and offer it up as a sacrifice.

But because Jesus was nailed to the cross, shed His blood for us, and gave the eternal sacrifice (Hebrews 10:10), we don't need to kill and sacrifice animals any more. We simply need to accept Jesus Christ with faith, and we can receive forgiveness for our sins. The sour wine represents the Law of the Old Testament, and new wine represents the grace of salvation through Jesus Christ. So in order to give us this new wine, Jesus Himself had taken the sour wine in our place.

Jesus was thirsty because He shed His blood. He felt thirsty because He had shed His holy blood to save us. So in order to quench the Lord's thirst, we need to discover the true value of His blood. We need to lead all the people—whose lives Jesus bought and paid for with His blood—to the way of salvation. After drinking the sour wine, Jesus confessed, "It is finished!" This means that He destroyed the wall of sin between God and man, and that He completed the way of salvation. After completely fulfilling His mission, Jesus cried out: *"Father, into Your hands I commit My spirit"* (Luke 23:46).

After saying this, He dropped His head and breathed His last. This was expressed in the Scripture as, "He gave up His spirit." This signifies that as the Savior who completed the way of salvation, Jesus would return to His glorious position.

The Four Gospels record all the words that Jesus said until He died on the cross. These words are called 'The Last Seven Words on the Cross' and each of these words contain deep, spiritual meanings. The disciples and the women at the foot of the cross who could only look on as Jesus died, cried and mourned bitterly. One of them was Mary Magdalene, who cried and comforted the Virgin Mary.

"Lord, who is more precious to me than my own life...
Lord, who gave me new life and guided me thus far...
I was as good as dead, and I had no life.
But I met You, and received new life.
You freed me from my suffering
and led me to live as a true person.
Lord, how can You be up there?
How can You be suffering up there?
Lord, I cannot live without You.
If only I can save the blood
You are shedding up there...
If only I can take Your suffering upon myself...
How can I comfort Your pain?
How can I share in Your suffering?
Lord, why will You die like this?"

Mary Magdalene cried bitterly at the foot of the cross

because she felt so helpless; for all she could do was just watch Jesus' suffering. Although she was but a frail woman, and she had no power to do anything, except to shed her tears, but her love for Jesus was like none other. The true love in her heart moved God's heart. This is how she later received the blessing of being the first person to meet the Lord after His resurrection.

Jesus Is Interred in a Tomb

It was around 3 in the afternoon when Jesus died. At this time, the sun lost its light, so there was darkness everywhere. The ground shook, and boulders burst open. One could actually feel the anguish and sorrow that God felt towards mankind's evil. At the same time Jesus passed away, the veil of the Temple was torn in two, from top to bottom (Luke 23:44-45).

The 'veil of the Temple' is the curtain that divides the Sanctuary and the Holy of Holies. Because the Sanctuary is where God's presence was, the average person could not go inside of it. Moreover, the Holy of Holies was a place only the high priest could go in once a year. The fact that this veil of the Temple was torn in two symbolizes how Jesus destroyed the wall of sin by becoming the atoning sacrifice. This is why

:: Jesus' last course and memorial church

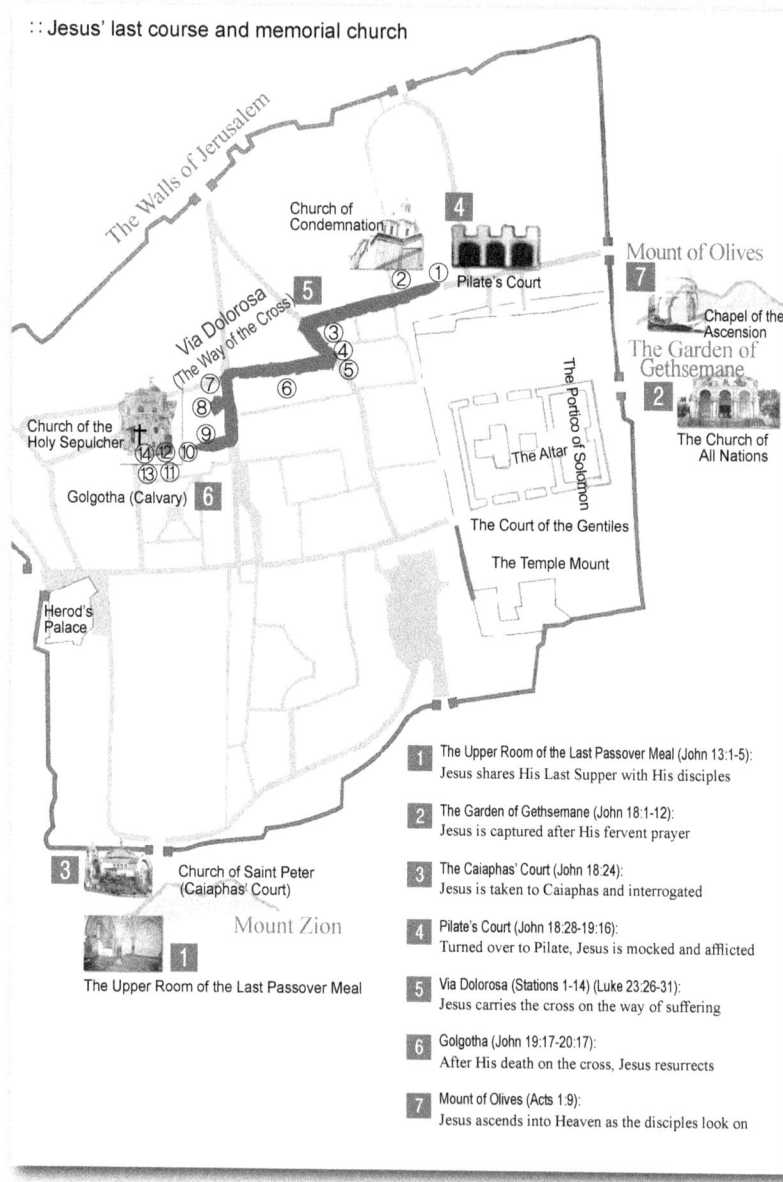

The Walls of Jerusalem

Church of Condemnation

4

Pilate's Court

Mount of Olives

7

Chapel of the Ascension

The Garden of Gethsemane

5

Via Dolorosa (The Way of the Cross)

③
④
⑤

2

⑦
⑧
⑨
⑥

The Church of All Nations

Church of the Holy Sepulcher

⑭⑫⑩
⑬⑪

Golgotha (Calvary)   6

The Portico of Solomon

The Altar

The Court of the Gentiles

The Temple Mount

Herod's Palace

3

Church of Saint Peter (Caiaphas' Court)

Mount Zion

1

The Upper Room of the Last Passover Meal

1 The Upper Room of the Last Passover Meal (John 13:1-5):
Jesus shares His Last Supper with His disciples

2 The Garden of Gethsemane (John 18:1-12):
Jesus is captured after His fervent prayer

3 The Caiaphas' Court (John 18:24):
Jesus is taken to Caiaphas and interrogated

4 Pilate's Court (John 18:28-19:16):
Turned over to Pilate, Jesus is mocked and afflicted

5 Via Dolorosa (Stations 1-14) (Luke 23:26-31):
Jesus carries the cross on the way of suffering

6 Golgotha (John 19:17-20:17):
After His death on the cross, Jesus resurrects

7 Mount of Olives (Acts 1:9):
Jesus ascends into Heaven as the disciples look on

anyone who believes in Jesus Christ can now go into the Temple and worship, and also pray directly to God (Hebrews 10:19-20).

The Reason Jesus' Legs Were Not Broken

"Then the Jews, because it was the day of preparation, so that the bodies would not remain on the cross on the Sabbath (for that Sabbath was a high day), asked Pilate that their legs might be broken, and that they might be taken away. So the soldiers came, and broke the legs of the first man and of the other who was crucified with Him; but coming to Jesus, when they saw that He was already dead, they did not break His legs" (19:31-33).

The day Jesus was crucified was the day of preparation. The 'day of preparation' was Friday, so it was a day to prepare for the Sabbath. The Sabbath day was a holy day, so no one could do any type of labor that day. According to the Law, it was not lawful to leave a body hanging on a tree over night. So the Jews went to Pilate and asked him to break the legs of the criminals on the cross.

According to Roman custom, a criminal's dead body was left on the cross as a warning to other people. That is why the Jews had to receive permission from Pilate before doing anything to the crucified bodies. Criminals that were crucified took a long time to die, because they could slightly depend on their feet to relieve the tension in their arms and chest. However, if their legs were broken, their circulation was cut off immediately, and due to difficulty breathing and renal failure, they died much more quickly.

At Pilate's command, the soldiers broke the legs of the two criminals on either side of Jesus. When they went to Jesus and saw that He had already died, they did not break His legs. There is a spiritual significance here as well. Jesus died on the cross as part of God's providence, not because He sinned. Therefore His bones could not be broken like those of criminals.

As it is written in Psalm 34:20, *"He keeps all his bones, not one of them is broken,"* God made sure His bones were not broken. This is the same reason God told the Israelites to eat the lamb, but not to break any of its bones (Exodus 12:46; Numbers 9:12). A lamb is a symbol for Jesus, who was without any spot or blemish.

The Reason Jesus Was Pierced in His Side and Had to Shed All of His Water and Blood

"But one of the soldiers pierced His side with a spear, and immediately blood and water came out. And he who has seen has testified, and his testimony is true; and he knows that he is telling the truth, so that you also may believe. For these things came to pass to fulfill the Scripture, 'Not a bone of Him shall be broken.' And again another Scripture says, 'They shall look on Him whom they pierced'" (19:34-37).

Even after confirming that Jesus had already died, one of the soldiers took a spear and pierced His side. Even if he did this just to check if Jesus was really dead, we can see man's evil nature here. From the side that was pierced by the sharp spear came a gush of water and blood. This was evidence that Jesus came in the form of man.

Even though He was not conceived from the bloodline of man, He came into this world in the complete form of man—in the form of creation. And, to the moment He breathed His last breath, He completely fulfilled His mission. Although by origin He is one with God, He came into this world in the body of a man and confirmed His love for us to the point of shedding all the blood and water from His own body.

There is yet another spiritual significance in the fact that Jesus shed all of His blood and water. Blood symbolizes life (Leviticus 17:14), and water symbolizes God's Word. Therefore Jesus shedding His blood and water symbolizes how He redeemed all mankind with His life and God's Word, thereby obliterating the wall of sin between God and man. And because of this sacrifice, we are not only freed from sin, but from all the curses that come from sin, like illnesses, tests, and tribulations.

To the eyes of the flesh, it appears as though a terrible and horrific thing happened to a young man named Jesus, who was crucified and pierced in the side with a spear. However, to spiritual eyes, this was an event that bore the complete fruit of God's love. The words of the Bible are true, and they are the truth. All Scripture is inspired by God (2 Timothy 3:16). Therefore all the words of the Old and New Testaments pair perfectly together in couplets, and all the prophecies have either already been fulfilled, or will be fulfilled (Isaiah 34:16).

It is written in verse 37, "And again another Scripture says, 'They shall look on Him whom they pierced.'" In Revelation 1:7 it is recorded, *"Behold, He is coming with the clouds, and every eye will see Him, even those who pierced Him; and all the tribes of the earth will mourn over Him. So it is to be. Amen."* Furthermore, "They shall look on Him whom they pierced," signifies the fact that they will see the resurrected Lord once again, and also that the Lord will return in the last day. Therefore the plan and providence of salvation through Jesus Christ is not only perfect in its timing, but it has also been configured elaborately and perfectly.

Joseph of Arimathea, Who Prepared the Tomb for Jesus

"After these things Joseph of Arimathea, being a disciple of Jesus, but a secret one for fear of the Jews, asked Pilate that he might take away the body of Jesus; and Pilate granted permission. So he came and took away His body" (19:38).

As soon as Jesus was sentenced to crucifixion, not only His disciples, but most of those who followed Him hid in fear. Therefore, in order to preserve the body of His beloved Son, God inspired a man who experienced His grace to prepare for His burial. First, He had Joseph of Arimathea prepare a tomb to place the body of Jesus. The Bible called him a rich man (Matthew 27:57), a prominent member of the Council, and one who was waiting for the kingdom of God (Mark 15:43). He was also a good and righteous man, who did not consent when the Sanhedrin conspired to capture and kill Jesus (Luke 23:50-51).

It was not easy for a member of the Sanhedrin to openly say he was a disciple of Jesus. The Jews had already decided to put out of the synagogue anyone who professed that Jesus was the Christ (John 9:22). That is why as the Scripture said, "Joseph of Arimathea, being a disciple of Jesus, but a secret one for fear of the Jews," Joseph did not openly disclose the fact that he was a disciple. We can see how hostile the atmosphere must have been at that time, for anyone who believed Jesus was the Savior.

Even though Joseph of Arimathea hid the fact that he was a disciple of Jesus, he could not just ignore Jesus' death. This is why he volunteered to carry out His burial. So he discreetly went to Pilate and asked for the body of Jesus (Mark 15:43). Pilate, who was still extremely uncomfortable about the death of Jesus, granted Joseph permission with ease.

Nicodemus, Who Prepared the Spices for the Burial

"Nicodemus, who had first come to Him by night, also came, bringing a mixture of myrrh and aloes, about a hundred pounds weight. So they took the body of Jesus and bound it in linen wrappings with the spices, as is the burial custom of the Jews. Now in the place where He was crucified there was a garden, and in the garden a new tomb in which no one had yet been laid. Therefore because of the Jewish day of preparation, since the tomb was nearby, they laid Jesus there" (19:39-42).

Besides Joseph of Arimathea, there was another man who prepared for Jesus' burial. It was Nicodemus, a member of the Jewish ruling Council. He first came to Jesus early and heard Him speak about being 'born again', after which he came to acknowledge that Jesus was a man of God, and later defended Him (John 3:7). He brought a mixture of myrrh and aloes, weighing about a hundred pounds, and wrapped Jesus' body with the linen and spices. Wrapping a body with linen and spices and placing the body in a cave for a tomb was a Jewish burial custom.

The amount of spices Nicodemus brought was equivalent to that used for a royal burial. He believed from the center of his heart that Jesus was more valuable than any king of this world. A tomb that was never used before was near the place of crucifixion. We can see God's love and provision here as well. Preparing in advance, the people who had received His grace, God made sure Jesus' burial was prepared and done completely, and well.

We must look back at ourselves and see if we also can do what Joseph of Arimathea and Nicodemus did. Joseph of Arimathea and Nicodemus were members of the Council; therefore it would have been very difficult for them to openly do what they did, due to their positions. If they thought about the negative consequences they would face, they could not have done anything because of fear. However, because of the grace they received from Jesus, and because they loved Him, they were able to be bold. In serving God, and the Lord, they did not seek for their own benefit, or incorporate their fleshly thoughts. Instead, they only acted out of true faith and love.

Chapter 20

Jesus, Who Resurrected

The People Who Came
to Visit the Empty Tomb

The Four Gospels record the ministry of Jesus, but each Gospel has its unique features. The only slight difference comes from the different *perspective* of the writers who were inspired by the Holy Spirit. Besides this fact, all the information recorded in the Gospels is the absolute truth. For example, the apostle John, who wrote the Gospel of John, wrote about the resurrection centered around Mary Magdalene. This was because he knew very well, how much Mary Magdalene loved the Lord, and how much the Lord loved her.

In the Gospel of Matthew, it is written that "Mary Magdalene and the other Mary" went to visit the tomb (Matthew 28:1), and the Gospel of Luke simply calls them "the women" (Luke 23:55). So when we put all these recordings together, we get a clearer picture about what happened.

Mary Magdalene Was the First to Discover the Empty Tomb

> "Early on the first day of the week, while it was still dark, Mary Magdalene went to the tomb and saw that the stone had been removed from the entrance. So she came running to Simon Peter and the other disciple, the one Jesus loved, and said, 'They have taken the Lord out of the tomb, and we don't know where they have put Him!'" (20:1-2)

The people who believed in Jesus and followed Him were greatly traumatized when Jesus was crucified, so they couldn't help but feel bitter. Mary Magdalene, the virgin Mary, and several other women were at the foot of the cross where Jesus died. Overcome by sorrow, they could not leave the cross. So they stayed there and watched as Joseph of Arimathea took Jesus' body, prepared for His burial, and laid Him in the tomb (Luke 23:50-55).

Because the next day was the Sabbath, Joseph of Arimathea, who was a member of the Council, decided to take matters into his own hands. When Nicodemus came with the spices, the two men wrapped the body with the linen and the spices and placed Jesus' body in a new tomb nearby. After the burial, Joseph moved a big rock in front of the entrance to the tomb. This is when the women came to their senses and left the place in a hurry to go buy the spices and perfumes to put on Jesus' body. They rushed away, because in a little while, the day would end, and the Sabbath day would begin, which means they would not be able to buy or sell anything.

Because their hearts were completely preoccupied by Jesus, who died, the women didn't even know how they spent their Sabbath. A few women quickly prepared to go to the tomb before twilight of the first day after the Sabbath. But to the women who were worried about how they were going to move the big boulder standing in front of the tomb, an unbelievable scene was waiting for them. Who moved the boulder, no one knew, but the entrance to the tomb was already opened.

After being shocked at the opened tomb, Mary Magdalene and the women approached to look inside the tomb, and they did not see Jesus' body. At that moment, two angels covered with bright, brilliant lights appeared before them. *"Why do you look for the living One among the dead? He is not here, but He has risen!"* (Luke 24:5-6)

The women heard from the angels that Jesus had risen from the dead, but they were so shocked they didn't quite understand what the angels meant. Simply awestruck from seeing the brilliant angels and finding Jesus' body gone from the tomb, they ran right down from the place, half in a daze. Mary Magdalene found Peter and John and told them this news: "They have taken the Lord out of the tomb, and we don't know where they have put Him!"

What Mary said was enough to shock both Peter and John. Yes, Jesus did tell His disciples that He would die, and then resurrect on the third day (Matthew 17:22-23). However, after actually witnessing Jesus' death, they were all so traumatized that they were not able to remember what Jesus had said. They really thought that someone must have stolen Jesus' body.

Peter and John Check the Empty Tomb

"So Peter and the other disciple went forth, and
they were going to the tomb. The two were running
together; and the other disciple ran ahead faster than
Peter and came to the tomb first; and stooping and
looking in, he saw the linen wrappings lying there;
but he did not go in. And so Simon Peter also came,
following him, and entered the tomb; and he saw
the linen wrappings lying there, and the face-cloth
which had been on His head, not lying with the linen
wrappings, but rolled up in a place by itself. So the
other disciple who had first come to the tomb then also
entered, and he saw and believed" (20:3-8).

Hearing the news from Mary Magdalene, Peter and John
ran to the tomb. John, who was faster than Peter, got to the
tomb first. He looked inside the tomb. He couldn't see the
body, but only the linen wrappings that were lying there.

Peter, out of breath, arrived a little later, and went right into
the tomb. No matter how hard he looked, he only saw the linen
wrappings and the face-cloth. The strange part was that the
linen wrappings and the face-cloth were not in the same place.
The face-cloth was neatly rolled in its own place. John then
came in after Peter and witnessed the same scene.

The fact that the face-cloth was neatly rolled up clearly

proves that the Lord resurrected. If someone had actually stolen the body of Jesus, just as the Jewish officials had feared, they would not have had the chance to leave the tomb in such a neat condition. They would have either just taken the body with the linen wrappings still covering it; or if they had removed the wrappings, they would have done it in such a rush that they would have left the tomb in a disarray, leaving linen wrappings all over the place. But the inside of the tomb, the way Peter and John saw it, was rather tranquil and neat.

"For as yet they did not understand the Scripture, that He must rise again from the dead. So the disciples went away again to their own homes" (20:9-10).

Psalm 16:10 says, *"For You will not abandon my soul to Sheol; nor will You allow Your Holy One to undergo decay."* The disciples did not know that this was a prophecy about Jesus' resurrection. They realized this only after they met the risen Lord in person. The Lord's resurrection is not only prophesied in the Old Testament, but Jesus actually spoke about it as well. But the disciples were shocked and worried, based on the situation they saw simply with their physical eyes.

Pilate's report to the Roman Emperor Caesar gives a detailed description about this event.

"The day after He was buried one of the priests came to the Praetorium and said they were so apprehensive that His disciples intended to steal the body of Jesus

and hide it, and then make it appear that He had risen from the dead, as He had foretold, and of which they were perfectly convinced. I sent him to the captain of the royal guard (Malcus) to tell him to take the Jewish soldiers, place as many around the sepulcher as were needed; then if anything should happen they could blame themselves and not the Romans.

When the great excitement arose about the sepulcher being found empty, I felt a deeper solicitude than ever. I sent for this man Islam, who related to me as near as I can recollect the following circumstances. They saw a soft and beautiful light over the sepulcher. He, at first, thought that the women had come to embalm the body of Jesus, as was their custom, but he could not see how they had gotten through the guards. While these thoughts were passing through his mind, behold the whole place was lightened up and there seemed to be crowds of the dead in their grave clothes.

All seemed to be shouting and filled with ecstasy, while all around and above was the most beautiful music he had ever heard and the whole air seemed to be full of voices praising God. All this time there seemed to be a reeling and swimming of the earth that he seemed to sicken and faint and he could not stand on his feet. He said the earth seemed to swim from under him, and his senses left him, so he knew not just what did occur.

I asked him what condition he was in when he came

to himself. He said he was lying on the ground with his face down. I asked him if his dizziness might not have come from being wakened up and getting up too suddenly as it sometimes has that effect. He said he had not been asleep, as the penalty was death to sleep on duty. He said some of the soldiers slept at a time and some were asleep then. I asked him how long the scene lasted. He said he did not know, but he thought nearly an hour. I asked him if he went to the sepulcher after he had come to himself. He said no; because he was afraid that just as soon as relief came they would go to their quarters.

I asked him if he had been questioned by the priests. He said he had. They wanted him to say it was an earthquake, and that they were asleep, and offered him money if he would say the disciples came and stole Jesus, but he saw no disciples and he did not know that the body was gone until he was told."

The Lord's resurrection is not a story the disciples or Christians made up. It was true, historic event. After resurrecting, Jesus showed Himself not only to Mary Magdalene, but to Peter, and several disciples, and later to more than five hundred brothers all at the same time (1 Corinthians 15:6). Those disciples who witnessed the Lord's resurrection became one at heart, and did not fear death. Without fear, they spread the gospel of Jesus Christ and His resurrection, everywhere they went. This was because the resurrection of the Lord is life and strength itself.

The People Who Met the Risen Lord

Mary Magdalene followed Peter and John back to the tomb. Even after the two men returned to their home, unable to find any clues as to what happened, Mary could not leave the tomb. It was hard enough to accept Jesus' death. But now that His body was missing, how do you think she felt? She had come early in the morning to put balm on Jesus' body, and now that His body was gone, there was no way to comfort her empty and forlorn heart. So she just stood outside the tomb, crying and crying again.

> "But Mary was standing outside the tomb weeping; and so, as she wept, she stooped and looked into the tomb; and she saw two angels in white sitting, one at the head and one at the feet, where the body of Jesus

had been lying. And they said to her, 'Woman, why are you weeping?' She said to them, 'Because they have taken away my Lord, and I do not know where they have laid Him'" (20:11-13).

After some time of weeping, Mary stooped down to look inside the tomb one more time. For a moment, she doubted her eyes. Two angels dressed in white sat where Jesus' body was, one at the head, and one at the feet. The angels asked her: "Woman, why are you weeping?" Then, she said, "They have taken away my Lord, and I do not know where they have laid Him."

Here we can see Mary's state of mind. The only hope she had at this point was to honor Jesus by putting balm on His body. Other than this, there was nothing else she could do to repay Him for the grace she received from Him. But even this hope was now gone. Mary was so distressed that she couldn't even recognize the angels, let alone even imagine that Jesus had risen.

Mary Magdalene Meets the Risen Lord

"When she had said this, she turned around and saw Jesus standing there, and did not know that it was Jesus. Jesus said to her, 'Woman, why are you weeping? Whom are you seeking?' Supposing Him to be the gardener, she said to Him, 'Sir, if you have carried Him away, tell me where you have laid Him, and I will take Him away.' Jesus said to her, 'Mary!' She turned and said to Him in Hebrew, 'Rabboni!' (which means,

Teacher)" (20:14-16).

Quickly looking back, Mary saw the risen Lord, but she did not recognize Him. Then the Lord said to Mary, "Woman, why are you weeping? Whom are you seeking?" Overcome with grief and sorrow, she thought He was the gardener, and answered: "Sir, if you have carried Him away, tell me where you have laid Him, and I will take Him away." So when the Lord said, "Mary!" only then Mary recognized Him. She received the honor of being the first person to meet the risen Lord.

> "Jesus said to her, 'Stop clinging to Me, for I have not yet ascended to the Father; but go to My brethren and say to them, "I ascend to My Father and your Father, and My God and your God."' Mary Magdalene came, announcing to the disciples, 'I have seen the Lord,' and that He had said these things to her" (20:17-18).

Mary Magdalene still could not believe that the Lord resurrected. How could she express the joy of meeting the Lord whom she loved more than her own life once again? Uncontrollable tears ran down her cheeks. When Mary couldn't control her joy and tried to approach Jesus, He makes one request: "Stop clinging to Me, for I have not yet ascended to the Father; but go to My brethren and say to them, 'I ascend to My Father and your Father, and My God and your God.'"

After the Lord completed His calling as the Savior, He had to return to God. Because He completed everything, He had to go see the Father and then receive the glory prepared for Him, which was the proper order. But because He had not ascended up to Him yet, He said this to Mary and told her to tell the other disciples the news about His resurrection.

Then why did the risen Lord meet Mary even before meeting the Father? This was because Mary's love for the Lord, and her good heart was superior to all others. Many people meet the Lord, follow Him, and love Him, but everyone's inner heart and actions are different. Albeit a short time, compared to the disciples who hid in fear, Mary Magdalene was not even afraid of losing her own life. If she could have taken up the cross in the Lord's place, she probably would have. So receiving the glory of being the first person to meet the risen Lord was not a mere coincidence.

The apostle John recorded exactly what Mary Magdalene told him about her encounter with the risen Lord. However, she did not tell him every detail of the conversation she had with the Lord. Of the things that the Lord requested of her, she only told him about the very important things the disciples needed to know.

The Lord told Mary Magdalene to tell the disciples that He had resurrected, and He encouraged her to live as His witness until the designated time. And He promised that in due time, they would be able to meet once again. Mary couldn't hide her excitement, and everywhere she went, she shouted, "I saw the Lord! And this is what He told me!" But even then, the disciples could not believe wholeheartedly.

The Disciples Filled with Joy after Meeting the Resurrected Lord

"So when it was evening on that day, the first day of the week, and when the doors were shut where the disciples were, for fear of the Jews, Jesus came and stood in their midst and said to them, 'Peace be with you.' And when He had said this, He showed them both His hands and His side. The disciples then rejoiced when they saw the Lord" (20:19-20).

Since Jesus' body had disappeared, the disciples were afraid of how the Jews would react. The high priest and his crowd of followers had asked Pilate to have soldiers guard Jesus' tomb because they were worried that the disciples would steal Jesus' body. And the body disappeared, so what they feared would happen, happened. This was a situation where all the arrows would point at the disciples.

Around evening time, the disciples who were concerned about this situation gathered together. And just in case they be sought out by the Jews, they closed all the windows and locked the door tightly. It was then. The door was securely locked, but the Lord appeared in the midst of them. The disciples thought they were seeing the Lord's spirit (Luke 24:37). Then Jesus spoke to the disciples who were still filled with fear and trembling: "Peace be with you." And He continued: *"See My hands and My feet, that it is I Myself; touch Me and see, for a spirit does not have flesh and bones as you see that I have"* (Luke 24:39).

The disciples came back to their senses and approached the Lord. Seeing the scars from the nail-piercing on His hands and feet, and the scar in the side from the spear, the disciples knew it had to be the Lord. Only then did they confirm that it was the Lord, and rejoiced. There is a reason the Bible records the fact that the doors were securely locked. This was to teach us about the resurrected body, or the body's transformation after resurrection.

In 1 Corinthians 15:51-53 it states, *"Behold, I tell you a mystery; we will not all sleep, but we will all be changed, in a moment, in the twinkling of an eye, at the last trumpet; for the trumpet will sound, and the dead will be raised imperishable, and we will be changed. For this perishable must put on the imperishable, and this mortal must put on immortality."*

During the Lord's Second Advent in the air, instantly, all the people who believed in the Lord will be transformed and lifted up into the air. This is when our bodies will change into resurrected bodies that do not decay or perish. And with this body, we will celebrate the Seven-year Wedding Banquet in the air, and after the seven years, we will return to the earth and spend a thousand years here.

The resurrected body is the state of the spirit and soul being fused with an immortal body, so it is visible to the eye, and it can be touched by the hand. However, it is totally different from our bodies today. With the resurrected bodies, we can still breathe and eat, but because the bodies are immortal bodies, we will not be constrained by the space and substances of this world—we would be able to move about freely, wherever we want to go, without restraints. Closed doors or concrete walls will not limit us.

Regardless of gender or age of the person, his/her resurrected body will be at the beautiful age of 33 years, but we will be able to recognize each person. After spending the thousand years on earth and passing the judgment of the White Throne, we will each go to our designated places in Heaven, and then transform into perfected heavenly bodies.

The biggest difference between the resurrected body and the perfected heavenly body is that the heavenly body shows exactly how much glory and heavenly rewards the person received from God, and it also shows how much the person was sanctified during his lifetime on earth. This is because during the judgment of the White Throne, each person receives the rewards, glory, and power according to how he lived and acted here on earth. So just by looking at a person's perfected heavenly body, everyone can see how much the person loved God and lived according to His Word, which heavenly dwelling place they belong to, and how great their rewards and glory are.

The Lord Gave Us Hope of the Resurrection

"So Jesus said to them again, 'Peace be with you; as the Father has sent Me, I also send you.' And when He had said this, He breathed on them and said to them, 'Receive the Holy Spirit. If you forgive the sins of any, their sins have been forgiven them; if you retain the sins of any, they have been retained'" (20:21-23).

By appearing before the disciples with His resurrected body, He planted the hope of the resurrection in them. He also told them, "Receive the Holy Spirit," and gave them great power and authority. And that power was the power to forgive sins:

"If you forgive the sins of any, their sins have been forgiven them; if you retain the sins of any, they have been retained."

In order to save mankind from sin, Jesus hung on the cross, and He shed His sacred blood there. Because He experienced death without any sin, He destroyed the power of death, resurrected, and became the Savior. So people who become one with this Lord through faith move from death to life. The Lord opened the way of salvation completely for us. This is why the Lord has the power and authority to forgive sins. However, the Lord's disciples also have this power and authority to forgive sins in the name of Jesus Christ.

There is a proviso here. 1 John 1:7 says, *"But if we walk in the Light as He Himself is in the Light, we have fellowship with one another, and the blood of Jesus His Son cleanses us from all sin."* In order for Jesus' blood to cleanse us from our sin, we need to walk in the Light—which means we need to live according to God's Word.

"Because You Have Seen Me, Have You Believed?"

After meeting the risen Lord, many followers of Jesus begin to lead new lives. The fear they once had disappeared, and they are filled with the hope of the resurrection. The disciples, and the women who followed Jesus could not hide their excitement, and talked about the Lord wherever they went. Unfortunately, there was one person who hadn't yet met the risen Lord. And that person was Thomas, who was called Didymus.

Thomas Doubts the Lord's Resurrection

"But Thomas, one of the twelve, called Didymus, was not with them when Jesus came. So the other disciples were saying to him, 'We have seen the Lord!' But he said to them, 'Unless I see in His hands the imprint of the nails, and put my finger into the place of the nails, and put my hand into His side, I will not believe'" (20:24-25).

One day, Thomas met with the disciples and heard their excitement in the words, "We have seen the Lord!"

Even though those who had met the risen Lord were zealously sharing about what they saw, Thomas just couldn't believe. He rather spoke in a loud voice: "Unless I see in His hands the imprint of the nails, and put my finger into the place of the nails, and put my hand into His side, I will not believe."

Even though Thomas saw Jesus' actions and he was taught directly by Him, he only accepted the teachings with his head knowledge. He did not have spiritual faith. Otherwise, he wouldn't have shown such lack of his faith in such a bold way. Even if he couldn't really believe the other people's words, he probably would have at least expressed some positive words with the hopes that what they said was true. In this way, when one tries to understand the spiritual world with fleshly thoughts, it is only natural that there is a limit to what one can perceive, and misunderstandings are bound to arise.

Thomas' Repentance and Confession

"After eight days His disciples were again inside, and Thomas with them. Jesus came, the doors having been shut, and stood in their midst and said, 'Peace be with you.' Then He said to Thomas, 'Reach here with your finger, and see My hands; and reach here your hand and put it into My side; and do not be unbelieving, but believing.' Thomas answered and said to Him, 'My Lord and my God!' Jesus said to him, 'Because you have seen Me, have you believed? Blessed are they who did not see, and yet believed'" (20:26-29).

Eight days passed. The disciples were once again gathered in one place. This time, Thomas was with them. At this time, Thomas couldn't believe his eyes. Although the door was tightly closed, the Lord appeared. It was just as the other disciples had told him a few days earlier. "Peace be with you."

The Lord gave Thomas, who had so much doubt, a chance to believe. "Reach here with your finger, and see My hands; and reach here your hand and put it into My side; and do not be unbelieving, but believing."

Here we can feel the Lord's love once again. No matter how much a person doubts and does not believe because of his fleshly thoughts, He does not give up on him. He does whatever He can to help him have true faith. This is the heart of the Lord, and the heart of God. Therefore Thomas completely cast out his fleshly thoughts of the past, and confessed before the Lord: "My Lord and my God!"

The Lord encouraged him to have bigger faith. "Because you have seen Me, have you believed? Blessed are they who did not see, and yet believed."

Finally, like the other disciples, Thomas became a new person and lived a transformed life. With true faith, he faithfully took on the calling as an apostle. Not even fearing death, he went to India to spread the gospel, where he was later martyred.

Now then, what did the Lord mean when He said, "Blessed are they who did not see, and yet believed"? It has been about two thousand years since the Lord resurrected and ascended into heaven. Compared to the number of people who witnessed the resurrection, now there are countless more people who have not witnessed the resurrection. Despite the fact that they did not witness the resurrection firsthand, there are so many people who live looking up to Heaven with the hope of the resurrection!

The apostle Paul was one also who did not witness the Lord's resurrection with his eyes; and yet after meeting the Lord, he lived for the gospel and he served with all of his life. These are the kinds of people the Lord was talking about when He said they were blessed because they believed even though they did not see.

The Purpose of Recording the Gospel of John

"Therefore many other signs Jesus also performed in the presence of the disciples, which are not written in this book; but these have been written so that you may believe that Jesus is the Christ, the Son of God; and that believing you may have life in His name" (20:30-31).

Because God knows people's hearts and thoughts very well, He only had His people record in the Bible those events that could be guidelines for people's spiritual lives, and those events that could build up their faith. If the Bible recorded every detail of what Jesus did, because of the limited human mindset, instead of gaining more faith, people would build more obstacles for themselves, and rather distance themselves from the Bible.

Even among unbelievers today, there are those who think the Bible is just another type of myth, or a book of made-up stories. But if there were even more miraculous stories recorded in the Bible, what would happen? So knowing man's heart, God only had His people record in the Bible just the basic events that show Jesus' divine nature, and human nature. He was making sure that the people can first believe the fact that Jesus is the Son of God, and that He is the Christ.

However, when a person receives the Holy Spirit, he can understand beyond these things, and delve deeper into the spiritual realm. He can even come to understand deeper things about the spiritual world that are not all recorded in the Bible. By having greater fellowship with the Holy Spirit, who understands even the deepest heart of God, one can hear His voice and receive great teachings from Him. This is why time and time again, the Lord told His disciples to receive the Holy Spirit.

Chapter 21

The Lord's Love
for His Disciples

1. The Lord Appears at the Sea of Galilee
(21:1-14)

2. "Do You Love Me?"
(21:15-25)

The Lord Appears
at the Sea of Galilee

The disciples, who were hiding in Jerusalem to avoid the Jews, gained new strength after meeting the risen Lord. Because the Lord told them that He was going to Galilee (Mark 16:7), they quickly left for Galilee, to the region of Tiberias. Because many of the disciples were fishermen from that region, Galilee was a familiar place that gave them comfort.

"After these things Jesus manifested Himself again to the disciples at the Sea of Tiberias, and He manifested Himself in this way. Simon Peter, and Thomas called Didymus, and Nathanael of Cana in Galilee, and the sons of Zebedee, and two others of His disciples were together. Simon Peter said to them, 'I am going fishing.' They said to him, 'We will also come with you.'

They went out and got into the boat; and that night they caught nothing" (21:1-3).

The disciples arrived in Galilee and looked for the Lord, but could not find Him. They had twice met the risen Lord in Jerusalem, but they had yet to receive any special calling up to that point. While the disciples did not know exactly what kind of work they needed to do now, Peter said he was going fishing. Thomas, Nathanael, James, John, and two other disciples followed him.

The disciples spent the whole night in the boat, and yet they caught nothing. Before being called a disciple, Peter had worked as a fisherman for a long time, so he was a skilled fisherman. And the sons of Zebedee, James and John had lived out their lives helping their father doing boat work, so by nature, they knew exactly *when* the fish were caught, and where they were caught best. But strangely on that night, they could not catch any fish. Their knowledge and experience were useless.

"Cast the Net on the Right-Hand Side"

"But when the day was now breaking, Jesus stood on the beach; yet the disciples did not know that it was Jesus. So Jesus said to them, 'Children, you do not have any fish, do you?' They answered Him, 'No.' And He said to them, 'Cast the net on the right-hand side of the boat and you will find a catch.' So they cast, and then they were not able to haul it in because of the great number of fish" (21:4-6).

Pretty soon, the sky grew bright. The disciples, who had spent the night on the sea taking on the wind, were very tired. Just then, the Lord appeared before them a third time. Even though He stood at the seashore, the disciples did not recognize Him. So He called out to them and asked: "Children, you do not have any fish, do you?" "No," they replied. Not recognizing the Lord's voice, the disciples called out a simple answer.

"Cast the net on the right-hand side of the boat and you will find a catch." Even though the disciples did not recognize the Lord's voice, they simply obeyed. Then, the unexpected happened. Although they did not catch one fish all night long, this time, there were so many fish they lacked the strength to haul them all into the boat!

Just like this, with anything we do, we should not depend on our own strength and wisdom, but we should gain strength and power by obeying the words of the Lord. And as Jesus called Peter by saying, "I will make you a fisher of men," when it comes to the work of saving souls, this is especially true. No matter how great man's knowledge and wisdom may be, the knowledge and wisdom of the flesh has limitations.

Furthermore, when it comes to catching souls, we need to cast out the urge to do things with our own knowledge and power. We should have the humble attitude to depend only on the Lord, and we need to ask the Father God for His grace and power.

Peter and the Disciples Meet the Lord

"Therefore that disciple whom Jesus loved said to Peter, 'It is the Lord.' So when Simon Peter heard that it was the Lord, he put his outer garment on (for he was stripped for work), and threw himself into the sea. But the other disciples came in the little boat, for they were not far from the land, but about one hundred yards away, dragging the net full of fish. So when they got out on the land, they saw a charcoal fire already laid and fish placed on it, and bread" (21:7-9).

When everyone was using all their might to pull in the net full of fish, John, who was the 'disciple whom Jesus loved', recognized the Lord first, and he said to Peter, "It is the Lord!"

As soon as he heard what John said, Peter put on his outer garment and jumped into the sea. This was in part because of his quick spontaneity; but most importantly, it was because of his great desire to meet the Lord. He even forgot that they had taken the boat far out into the sea in order to catch fish. The boat was about one hundred yards from the land.

This is the same Peter who had denied Jesus three times because he was engulfed in his fleshly thoughts and he couldn't win over his fear. But after repenting wholeheartedly, he totally demolished his self-righteousness and fleshly thoughts. So the fact that Peter didn't even think twice before jumping into the water to follow the Lord shows this transformation in him. He had become a person who only focused on the Lord, without being swayed by any circumstances or situations.

The other disciples also rushed into the smaller boat with the net full of fish. When they got to the shore, they saw that a charcoal fire was already going, and fish cooking over it. There was even some bread to fill their hunger after the previous night's hard work.

> "Jesus said to them, 'Bring some of the fish which you have now caught.' Simon Peter went up and drew the net to land, full of large fish, a hundred and fifty-three; and although there were so many, the net was not torn" (21:10-11).

The Lord told the disciples to bring some of the fresh fish they had just caught. Without delay, Peter drew the net onto the land, and the other disciples began to help him. Here we can see how much the disciples changed after meeting the risen Lord.

Of course when they were with Jesus before, they did not fear anything, for Jesus had amazing power, but this was not due to their own faith. So when Jesus finally died on the cross, they could not surpass their own limiting power, and returned to being ordinary, average people again.

However, after meeting the resurrected Lord, they transformed. They rid themselves of the frameworks of their mind, and gained faith and obedience that came truly from their hearts. This time as well, they saw that there was enough fish and bread for all of them to eat, but when the Lord told them to bring more fish, they had faith that there was a good reason for the Lord's words. When they counted the fish Peter drew up, they saw that there were one hundred fifty-three large fish. Just the fact that the net did not tear was amazing in itself.

There is a spiritual significance here in the fact that the net did not tear, even though they pulled all the fish they caught with it. What we can learn from this is that the blessing that comes from the Lord is greater and more numerous than we can ever imagine, and this kind of blessing will never leak away.

3 John 1:2 says, *"Beloved, I pray that in all respects you may prosper and be in good health, just as your soul prospers,"* and in many other places in the Bible, God promises us that when we live according to God's Word, He will give us all kinds of blessings. The vessel with which to receive His blessings is prepared when we obey God's Word. Preparing this vessel means completely obeying God's Word, instead of doing whatever our mind desires to do.

The Lord Teaches About the Resurrected Body

"Jesus said to them, 'Come and have breakfast.' None of the disciples ventured to question Him, 'Who are You?' knowing that it was the Lord. Jesus came and took the bread and gave it to them, and the fish likewise. This is now the third time that Jesus was manifested to the disciples, after He was raised from the dead" (21:12-14).

Before arriving at Galilee, the disciples had met the resurrected Lord twice. This is hard to believe with the human mind, but after meeting the Lord, they came to believe completely in the resurrection. That is why when the Lord appeared to them again, they did not ask Him who He was.

The Lord gave the fish and bread to the disciples who had suffered all night long. We can feel the Lord's gentle and loving heart here. The reason why He did this was to show the disciples what the resurrected body is like. With the resurrected body, the moment a person eats something, it immediately becomes decomposed and leaves the body through the breath.

It also applies when after the judgment of the White Throne our resurrected bodies transform into perfected heavenly bodies and we live in Heaven with perfected heavenly bodies. In Heaven, people drink from the water of life, eat all kinds of different fruits, drink fragrances, and are happy. To drink fragrances means to smell wonderful fragrances. Of course one can live without eating in Heaven, but when one drinks in fragrances, he experiences greater joy and happiness, and his spirit becomes satisfied and refreshed. Just as people here feel satisfied and happy when they eat good food, people in Heaven also feel this way when they drink in the fragrances of all the different flowers and fruits. Just like putting on perfume, the fragrances enter the body and circulate throughout the whole body, so one becomes very filled and happy.

Not only did the Lord show the resurrected body so the disciples would have faith, but He added to their hope of Heaven so they can faithfully fulfill the calling they were about to be given. And by showing both His divine nature and His human nature, He made sure they felt His love, His mercy, and His warmth, so they could enjoy being in His embrace.

"Do You Love Me?"

For the disciples, spending that morning with the Lord by the Sea of Tiberias gave them more joy than any other time. Meeting the Lord over the period of three times, their faith increased, and they all came to have true faith. And through Peter, the Lord let the disciples know what they would have to do in the future. And through the conversation He had with Peter, we can feel the Lord's heart.

"Tend My Lambs"

"So when they had finished breakfast, Jesus said to Simon Peter, 'Simon, son of John, do you love Me more than these?' He said to Him, 'Yes, Lord; You know that

I love You.' He said to him, 'Tend My lambs'" (21:15).

After breakfast, the Lord asked Peter: "Simon, son of John, do you love Me more than these?" Even though there was a shameful time when he denied the Lord, now Peter had the perfect opportunity to confess how much he really loved the Lord. Peter said, "Yes, Lord; You know that I love You." After hearing Peter's confession, the Lord spoke to him: "Tend My lambs."

In Exodus chapter 12 there is a scene where the Israelites ate lambs. Before sending down His final curse of the death plague of the firstborns upon the Egyptians for going against God's words, He told the Israelites a way to avoid this plague. On the night of the plague, they were to slaughter a lamb, eat the meat by roasting it over the fire, and put its blood on the doorposts and the lintel of their homes. This would be a sign that God would not kill the people inside that house.

The lamb here symbolizes Jesus Christ (John 1:29; Revelations 5:6-8). And the blood of the lamb was a sign prophesying that the sacred blood of Jesus Christ would forgive mankind's sins so man can avoid death. What this means is that just as in the Old Testament during the Exodus times, the Israelites ate the lamb's meat and put its blood on the doorframe of their house, in the New Testament, one needs to eat the Lord's flesh and drink His blood in order to gain salvation and receive eternal life. To eat the Lord's flesh and drink His blood means to take God's Word as food for the heart, and keep His Word by living according to it (John 6:53).

So when the Lord told Peter to "Tend My lambs," He was

telling him to 'teach and spread the word of the Lord who is the Lamb of God, who is the way, the truth, and the life.' It means the Lord told him to teach and spread the Word of God that is leading us to blessing. The reason the Lord did not say, "Feed them God's words which I have taught you," but to 'Tend My lambs' was to teach them where they need to put their focus as they spread the gospel.

When we spread the gospel, the most important part of the gospel is the cross of salvation of the Lamb, Jesus Christ. We need to take in the fact that Jesus, who was without any sin, shed His sacred blood to save mankind, and we also need to take in the secret hidden in the cross, or the "message of the cross".

So believers who eat the 'Lamb' well, realize why Jesus is the Savior and gain faith, and true life comes into their hearts. Even if they happen to encounter hardship, they do not forget about the Lord's love, or walk away from their faith. This is why when evangelizing and tending to many souls, it is most important to feed them the 'Lamb' above all other worldly teachings.

"Shepherd My Sheep"

"He said to him again a second time, 'Simon, son of John, do you love Me?' He said to Him, 'Yes, Lord; You know that I love You.' He said to him, 'Shepherd My sheep'" (21:16).

The risen Lord asked the same question to Peter once again.

"Simon, son of John, do you love Me?"
"Yes, Lord; You know that I love You."
"Shepherd My sheep"

Frequently, the Bible compares 'children of God', or 'believers' to 'sheep'. Isaiah 53:6 says, *"All of us like sheep have gone astray, each of us has turned to his own way; but the LORD has caused the iniquity of us all to fall on Him,"* and Mark 6:34 states, *"When Jesus went ashore, He saw a large crowd, and He felt compassion for them because they were like sheep without a shepherd; and He began to teach them many things."*

A shepherd will tend to his sheep by leading them to quiet waters and green pastures. He protects them from danger and leads them to the right way and helps them grow and mature well. Servants or stewards of the Lord, who have received the calling from the Lord, who is the Chief Shepherd, are like small shepherds. These people need to diligently feed their sheep with God's Word so their faith grows, and they need to protect their sheep with prayer so that even if temptations come their way, the sheep can have victory through faith.

So just as the Lord first said, "Tend My lambs," we need to clearly teach the message of the cross, and when they receive assurance of salvation, just as the Lord said, "Shepherd my sheep," the next thing we need to do is to lead the believers to grow in faith so they become choice grains of wheat.

"Tend My Sheep"

> "He said to him the third time, 'Simon, son of John, do you love Me?' Peter was grieved because He said to him the third time, 'Do you love Me?' And he said to Him, 'Lord, You know all things; You know that I love You.' Jesus said to him, 'Tend My sheep'" (21:17).

The Lord asked Peter the same question three times. "Do you love Me?" Not realizing the Lord's intention and spiritual meaning of His question, Peter became a little disturbed. Of course he wasn't disturbed because of some evil heart or because he was offended. He was disturbed because even though he loved the Lord from the center of his heart, he had to acknowledge that he still had many weaknesses.

"Lord, You know all things; You know that I love You."
"Tend My sheep."

Once in a while there are people who say maybe the Lord asked Peter three times because Peter once denied Him three times. However, the Lord of love does not pierce one's heart with past wrongs when one has repented and turned away from the wrong. As it is written in Psalm 103:12, *"As far as the east is from the west, so far has He removed our transgressions from us,"* as long as we repented of our sins, He doesn't even remember it. Then why did the Lord ask Peter to "Tend My sheep"?

A person who has received Jesus Christ not only begins leading a renewed life, but his faith also matures and grows. But not everyone is the same. There are some souls that grow very well, and there are some souls that are slow to change, fall into temptation, fade away, or become offended and wither. The Lord's last request was His way of telling Peter not to lose strength or give up even though he comes across these types of souls, and diligently pursue feeding them the truth.

Through the Lord's repeated questions and strong encouragement, we can discover the Lord's instructions for just how His disciples should take on their callings. First, disciples need to teach the souls about God and Jesus Christ and lead them to salvation. Then they need to help them mature in their faith so they become choice wheat. And even if some souls fade away or become withered, they should not give up on them, but continue to lead them with diligence. The Lord wanted to make sure many people become God's children; that is why He asked Peter to 'Tend My sheep' three times—so he understands and remembers in his heart, just how important this calling is.

This moment was a very special time for Peter, because it was the turning point of his life. He inscribed in his heart, the conversation he had with the Lord that day, and cherished it for years to come. As a result, he was able to fulfill his calling powerfully. After understanding the Lord's heart, Peter dedicated his life to saving souls, and in the end, he finished his life as a martyr.

The Lord did not ask Peter the same question three times because He didn't know Peter's heart. He knew how much Peter loved Him, and He knew how much passion he had for

His ministry. But by making him confess with his mouth, He was making Peter inscribe his calling completely in his heart. Although Jesus asked only Peter this question, the same question applied to all the disciples. Not only that, it also applies to all the Lord's servants until the Lord's return, and to all the children of God who received His blessing of salvation first.

"Follow Me!"

> "'Truly, truly, I say to you, when you were younger, you used to gird yourself and walk wherever you wished; but when you grow old, you will stretch out your hands and someone else will gird you, and bring you where you do not wish to go.' Now this He said, signifying by what kind of death he would glorify God. And when He had spoken this, He said to him, 'Follow Me!'" (21:18-19)

The Lord's teaching did not end here. He even told Peter what was to happen to him in the future. He told him that when he was young, he would gird himself and go wherever he pleased, but when he became old, he would be led by others to go where he did not want to go.

When the Lord used the words 'young' and 'old' here, He was not simply referring to a person's age. He was illustrating that while the days when Peter powerfully carries out his calling as the Lord's witness is the time he is 'young', the days when

Peter's calling comes to an end is the time he is 'old'.

A 'gird' is not just something one puts around the waist, but it is a symbol representing 'authority'. When the Lord talked about how Peter 'girded' himself when he was younger, the 'gird' here symbolizes the 'authority of God's Word', or the 'authority of believing in Jesus Christ'. So by saying 'Peter girded himself when he was younger and walked wherever he wanted to', means that Peter will take 'the authority of God', and 'the authority of God's Word' and go here and there witnessing the Lord. And when the Lord said that 'Peter would be girded by someone else and taken to a place he did not want to go when he becomes old', it means that when Peter's calling is fulfilled, 'the gird someone else puts on Peter', or 'the authority of this world' would lead to Peter's martyrdom.

However, Peter's martyrdom was not simply caused by the people who have authority of this world; it would occur in the midst of God's providence. Because Peter knew this will of God, he was able to obey with joy. "You will stretch out your hands" also signifies that Peter would receive his martyrdom without any resistance.

According to oral history, in the later years, while Peter was spreading the gospel in Rome, he decided to leave that place for a little while to avoid Emperor Nero's harsh persecutions. But when he was close to leaving Roman boundaries, he met the Lord. Peter was shocked, and asked: "Quo vadis, Domine (Lord, where are You going)?"

Then the Lord looked at him and said, "I am going to Rome to be crucified once again for My people." Peter quickly came to his senses and realized that it was the Lord's will for him to become martyred in Rome, so he turned back around. And finally, Peter was captured while spreading the gospel, and he was crucified to be a martyr. Before meeting the Lord, Peter lived trusting in his own wisdom and strength. But after becoming transformed, he lived a life that the Lord wanted—a life that glorified God.

When the Lord told Peter, "Follow Me," He was telling Peter to imitate the kind of life He led. In order to fulfill God's will, the Lord left all the glory of heaven to come to this world and He humbled Himself and submitted to the point of death. And the Lord was asking Peter and the other disciples to follow Him and also walk the path He walked.

But the Lord said, *"If anyone wishes to come after Me, he must deny himself, and take up his cross daily and follow Me"* (Luke 9:23). Just as the Lord stepped down from His glorious place as the Son of God and took on the flesh of a poor and lowly man, anyone who wants to follow the Lord must deny himself. The apostle Paul, as the apostle to the Gentiles, led many people to the way of salvation. He too, denied himself completely, confessing, *"I die daily"* (1 Corinthians 15:31).

Unimaginable glory is promised for people who truly deny themselves and follow the Lord like this. As it is written in John 12:26, *"If anyone serves Me, he must follow Me; and where I am, there My servant will be also; if anyone serves Me, the Father will honor him,"* even though the way of the cross is hard and difficult, it is the way to get to the glorious place where the Lord is. The Father God honors people who take up this way.

> "Peter, turning around, saw the disciple whom Jesus loved following them; the one who also had leaned back on His bosom at the supper and said, 'Lord, who is the one who betrays You?' So Peter seeing him said to Jesus, 'Lord, and what about this man?'" (21:20-21)

After listening to his calling, he noticed that the disciple whom Jesus loved was following them. The fact that John was 'following' them shows how much he loved and depended on the Lord, and how much he desired to obey His every word.

At the last supper, John was leaning against Jesus' bosom, and when Jesus was being crucified, he was at His feet, receiving Jesus' request to take care of the Virgin Mary. By these things, we can see just how close he was to Jesus. Suddenly, Peter became curious about John's calling. "Lord, and what about this man?" Because Peter believed that the Lord knew everything, he wanted to know in detail about John's calling as well.

> "Jesus said to him, 'If I want him to remain until I come, what is that to you? You follow Me!' Therefore this saying went out among the brethren that that disciple would not die; yet Jesus did not say to him that he would not die, but only, 'If I want him to remain until I come, what is that to you?'" (21:22-23).

Just as everyone's face is different, everyone's role is different, so each person's calling from God is different. Some people may

:: John Receives the Revelation at Patmos Island

be martyred, like Peter, and some people may not be martyred, like John. However, this does not mean one is more important than the other. This is why Jesus said about this, "What is that to you?"

A calling from God can neither be classified as big nor small. Every calling is important. The important thing is, no matter what the calling, we each need to take on the calling with the unchanging heart of Lord. In order to emphasize this attitude of the heart, the Lord said again, "You follow Me!"

Also, the reason the Lord said about John, "If I want him to remain until I come," was to show that he has a different calling from Peter. However, unlike the Lord's intention, these words were misinterpreted by the disciples that "that disciple would not die."

Yes, the apostle John is the only one among the disciples who was not martyred. However, at that time, Jesus was not simply talking about whether he would be martyred or not martyred, but that each person had a different calling. But because the listener did not understand His intention correctly, His words were passed on with a different meaning.

Therefore when we read the Bible, we need to be very cautious about points like these. If we interpret the Bible according to our own thoughts, we can build up many misconceptions. So it is very important not to understand the Bible based on the literal meaning of the words expressed in it, but to understand God's heart and intention that is captured within the words of the Bible through guidance of the Holy Spirit.

John detected the Lord's intention, so when he recorded this part, he wrote, "Yet Jesus did not say to him that he would not die, but only, 'If I want him to remain until I come, what is that to you?'" John understood Jesus' intention when He told Peter, "You follow Me." It was that He wanted Peter not to worry about other people's callings but to simply focus on following Him.

"And There Are Also Many Other Things Which Jesus Did"

"This is the disciple who is testifying to these

things and wrote these things, and we know that his testimony is true. And there are also many other things which Jesus did, which if they were written in detail, I suppose that even the world itself would not contain the books that would be written" (21:24-25).

The words of God that are recorded in the Bible are not stories made up by man's thoughts. The Bible records writings by people who received the words from God, as they were guided by the Holy Spirit. Therefore every word in the Bible is truth. The Gospel of John was also written by John in fullness of the Holy Spirit. It records information about the situations that took place at that time, exactly the way it took place. However, because he couldn't record every single detail about what Jesus did, he only took the core information and recorded them.

If the Bible was to record every detail of God's will and providence, and all the spiritual secrets, it would not be able to record everything—even if the skies were the parchment and the oceans were the ink. On top of that, there are many other secrets that cannot be expressed or understood by the language of this world.

This is why in each time period, He chose people who are pleasing to His heart to give them revelations about the deep, spiritual world. Ephesians 1:17 says, *"That the God of our Lord Jesus Christ, the Father of glory, may give to you a spirit of wisdom and of revelation in the knowledge of Him."* And Matthew 11:27 reads, *"And no one knows the Son except the Father; nor does anyone know the Father except the Son, and anyone to whom the Son wills to reveal Him."*

We have studied the footsteps of the Lord thus far. The Lord, who is one with God, came to this world to open the way of salvation, and He obeyed the very will of God so that His providence would be fulfilled. Philippians 2:6-8 states, *"Although He existed in the form of God, [He] did not regard equality with God a thing to be grasped, but emptied Himself, taking the form of a bond-servant, and being made in the likeness of men. Being found in appearance as a man, He humbled Himself by becoming obedient to the point of death, even death on a cross."*

The Lord has given us salvation and eternal life by overcoming death and resurrecting. More than 2,000 years later, His exalted life still transforms countless lives today, and helps them gain true life. I pray in the name of Jesus Christ that you, the reader, will follow the footsteps of the Lord as His witness in the end time, and become a valuable servant for His kingdom!

The Ascension and Another Helper

The Mount of Olives—as the name suggests, grand olive trees covering the mount provide shade all around. It's as if time has frozen, or died. And the green leaves that rise from the tops of the trees create a strange sense of tension in people. It's like death and life exist together here. After His resurrection, the Lord spent 40 days appearing before the disciples and teaching them about the work of God's kingdom. When it was time for His ascension, He went up to the Mount of Olives to give His loving disciples the last command.

Acts 1:4-5 reads, *"Gathering them together, He commanded them not to leave Jerusalem, but to wait for what the Father had promised, 'which,' He said, 'you heard of from Me; for John baptized with water, but you will be baptized with the Holy Spirit not many days from now.'"* More than anyone else, the disciples had gotten a firsthand look at the

Lord's life. Not only did they see signs and wonders that only God could perform, but they also experienced the Lord's suffering on the cross, death, and finally His resurrection—all as direct witnesses. After completing His mission as the Savior, the Lord saw with faith that countless souls would come to receive salvation through His loving disciples.

"Go into all the world and preach the gospel to all creation. He who has believed and has been baptized shall be saved; but he who has disbelieved shall be condemned. These signs will accompany those who have believed: in My name they will cast out demons, they will speak with new tongues; they will pick up serpents, and if they drink any deadly poison, it will not hurt them; they will lay hands on the sick, and they will recover" (Mark 16:15-18).

"And behold, I am sending forth the promise of My Father upon you; but you are to stay in the city until you are clothed with power from on high" (Luke 24:49).

"But you will receive power when the Holy Spirit has come upon you; and you shall be My witnesses both in Jerusalem, and in all Judea and Samaria, and even to the remotest part of the earth" (Acts 1:8).

After giving His last command, the Lord took the disciples out to Bethany, raised His hands and blessed them; then

He left them and ascended into heaven (Luke 24:50-51). Awestruck by the great scene before them, the disciples were not able to close their mouths. Covered by clouds the Lord was no longer visible. While the disciples were looking intently into the sky, two angels clothed in white came before them: *"Men of Galilee, why do you stand looking into the sky? This Jesus, who has been taken up from you into heaven, will come in just the same way as you have watched Him go into heaven"* (Acts 1:11).

The disciples who witnessed the Lord's ascension returned to Jerusalem with joy and became one at heart, praying together, and waiting for the promised Holy Spirit. On the day of the Pentecost, they were gathered together praying, as before, and a strong and quick wind came from heaven, and the Holy Spirit, like fire, came to rest upon each person. Their whole bodies became hot, and they experienced a fullness they had never experienced before. In fullness of the Holy Spirit, they each spoke different languages as the Spirit enabled them, and the disciples who received the power of the Holy Spirit went to the ends of the earth to be the Lord's witnesses.

With one sermon, the apostle Peter brought three thousand souls to repentance, and when he commanded in the name of Jesus Christ, a man who had been crippled from birth rose up, walked, and leaped. People even carried the sick out into the streets and laid them on cots and pallets, so that when Peter came by at least his shadow might fall on any one of them.

Although in the apostle Paul's case, he met the Lord later on, after receiving the power of the Holy Spirit, he was unharmed even after being bitten by a poisonous snake, and he even raised a dead person to life. When people took his handkerchiefs and aprons and put them on the sick, they were healed.

These kinds of works of the Holy Spirit still continue on today through the Lord's witnesses who have received the power of the Holy Spirit. And as the end time draws near, more miraculous events are taking place. Now the one thing we must be clear about is the fact that the Lord who ascended into heaven will return again in the same way. We need to be awake and live as His witnesses, according to the Great Commission, and we need to prepare to receive the Lord by following in His footsteps—keeping ourselves pure and holy.

"The Lord is not slow about His promise, as some count slowness, but is patient toward you, not wishing for any to perish but for all to come to repentance" (2 Peter 3:9).

"Go therefore and make disciples of all the nations, baptizing them in the name of the Father and the Son and the Holy Spirit, teaching them to observe all that I commanded you; and lo, I am with you always, even to the end of the age" (Matthew 28:19-20).

"Amen. Come, Lord Jesus" (Revelation 22:20).

The Author
Dr. Jaerock Lee

Dr. Jaerock Lee was born in Muan, Jeonnam Province, Republic of Korea, in 1943. While in his twenties, Dr. Lee suffered from a variety of incurable diseases for seven years and awaited death with no hope for recovery. However one day in the spring of 1974 he was led to a church by his sister and when he knelt down to pray, the living God immediately healed him of all his diseases.

From the moment he met the living God through that wonderful experience, Dr. Lee has loved God with all his heart and sincerity, and in 1978 he was called to be a servant of God. He prayed fervently with countless fasting prayers so that he could clearly understand the will of God, wholly accomplish it and obey the Word of God. In 1982, he founded Manmin Central Church in Seoul, Korea, and countless works of God, including miraculous healings, signs and wonders, have been taking place at his church ever since.

In 1986, Dr. Lee was ordained as a pastor at the Annual Assembly of Jesus' Sungkyul Church of Korea, and four years later in 1990, his sermons began to be broadcast in Australia, Russia, and the Philippines. Within a short time many more countries were being reached through the Far East Broadcasting Company, the Asia Broadcast Station, and the Washington Christian Radio System.

Three years later, in 1993, Manmin Central Church was selected as one of the "World's Top 50 Churches" by the Christian World magazine (US) and he received an Honorary Doctorate of Divinity from Christian Faith College, Florida, USA, and in 1996 he received his Ph. D. in Ministry from Kingsway Theological Seminary, Iowa, USA.

Since 1993, Dr. Lee has been spearheading world evangelization through many overseas crusades in Tanzania, Argentina, L.A., Baltimore City, Hawaii, and New York City of the USA, Uganda, Japan, Pakistan, Kenya, the Philippines, Honduras, India, Russia, Germany, Peru, Democratic Republic of the Congo, Israel and Estonia.

In 2002 he was acknowledged as a "worldwide revivalist" for his powerful ministries in various overseas crusades by major Christian newspapers in

Korea. In particular was his 'New York Crusade 2006' held in Madison Square Garden, the most famous arena in the world. The event was broadcast to 220 nations, and in his 'Israel United Crusade 2009', held at the International Convention Center (ICC) in Jerusalem he boldly proclaimed Jesus Christ is the Messiah and Savior.

His sermons are broadcast to 176 nations via satellites including GCN TV and he was listed as one of the 'Top 10 Most Influential Christian Leaders' of 2009 and 2010 by the popular Russian Christian magazine In Victory and news agency Christian Telegraph for his powerful TV broadcasting ministry and overseas church-pastoring ministry.

As of May of 2013, Manmin Central Church has a congregation of more than 120,000 members. There are 10,000 branch churches world-wide including 56 domestic branch churches, and more than 129 missionaries have been commissioned to 23 countries, including the United States, Russia, Germany, Canada, Japan, China, France, India, Kenya, and many more so far.

As of the date of this publishing, Dr. Lee has written 85 books, including bestsellers *Tasting Eternal Life before Death, My Life My Faith I & II, The Message of the Cross, The Measure of Faith, Heaven I & II, Hell, Awaken, Israel!,* and *The Power of God.* His works have been translated into more than 75 languages.

His Christian columns appear on *The Hankook Ilbo, The JoongAng Daily, The Chosun Ilbo, The Dong-A Ilbo, The Munhwa Ilbo, The Seoul Shinmun, The Kyunghyang Shinmun, The Korea Economic Daily, The Korea Herald, The Shisa News,* and *The Christian Press.*

Dr. Lee is currently leader of many missionary organizations and associations. Positions include: Chairman, The United Holiness Church of Jesus Christ; President, Manmin World Mission; Permanent President, The World Christianity Revival Mission Association; Founder & Board Chairman, Global Christian Network (GCN); Founder & Board Chairman, World Christian Doctors Network (WCDN); and Founder & Board Chairman, Manmin International Seminary (MIS).

Heaven I & II

A detailed sketch of the gorgeous living environment the heavenly citizens enjoy and beautiful description of different levels of heavenly kingdoms.

The Message of the Cross

A powerful awakening message for all the people who are spiritually asleep! In this book you will find the reason Jesus is the only Savior and the true love of God.

Hell

An earnest message to all mankind from God, who wishes not even one soul to fall into the depths of Hell! You will discover the never-before-revealed account of the cruel reality of the Lower Grave and Hell.

Tasting Eternal Life Before Death

A testimonial memoirs of Dr. Jaerock Lee, who was born again and saved from the valley of death and has been leading an exemplary Christian life.

The Measure of Faith

What kind of a dwelling place, crown and reward are prepared for you in Heaven? This book provides with wisdom and guidance for you to measure your faith and cultivate the best and most mature faith.

Awaken, Israel

Why has God kept His eyes on Israel from the beginning of the world to this day? What kind of His providence has been prepared for Israel in the last days, who await the Messiah?

My Life My Faith I & II

Dr. Jaerock Lee's autobiography provides the most fragrant spiritual aroma for the readers, through his life extracted from the love of God blossomed in midst of the dark waves, cold yoke and the deepest despair.

The Power of God

A must-read that serves as an essential guide by which one can possess true faith and experience the wondrous power of God